Overcomi

Six months of Faith-inspiring messages

Dan Chesney

New Wine Press

New Wine Press
P.O. Box 17
Chichester PO20 6RY
England

All quotations are from the New King James Bible unless otherwise stated.

New King James Version – Open Bible Expanded Edition
© Copyright 1983 Thomas Nelson Inc. Box 141000, Nashville, TN 37214 U.S.A.

Living Bible – Paraphrased
© Copyright 1971 Tyndale House Publishers, Wheaton, Illinois 60187 U.S.A.

Amplified Bible
© Copyright 1965 Zondervan Publishing House, Grand Rapids, Michigan MI 49506 U.S.A.

Riverside New Testament, William C. Ballantine
Houghton Mifflin Company, The Riverside Press, Cambridge 1923

Twentieth Century New Testament
© Copyright Fleming H. Revell, New York & Chicago 1902

The Cottonpatch Version of Paul's Epistles, Clarence Jordan
© Copyright 1968, Association Press, 291 Broadway, New York, NY 1007, U.S.A..

The Holy Bible in the Language of Today
An American Translation, William F. Beck.
A.J. Holman Company, division of J.B. Lippincott Company & Leaders Press
© Copyright Mrs William F. Beack 1976

The Letters of Paul, An Expanded Paraphrase, F.F. Bruce
© Copyright 1965 Wm B. Eerdman's Publishing Company, Grand Rapids, Michigan U.S.A.

The Letters of St. Paul, Arthur S. Way, M.A.
Macmillan & Co Limited, London & New York
The Macmillan Co. 1901

The Solid Rock, William B. Bradbury

A Shelter in the Time of Storm, Ira D. Sankey

What a Friend we have in Jesus, Charles C. Converse

Standing on the Promises, R. Kelso Carter
Living Way Hymnal ©1978 p.60
The International Church of the Foursquare Gospel
1100 Glendale Blvd. L.A., CA 90026 U.S.A.

Love Lifted Me, John T. Benson 1940
Used by permission of the Benson Co.
365 Circle Rd. Nashville, TN 37228, U.S.A., p.218.

ISBN 0 947852 49 2

Typeset by CRB Typesetting Services, Ely, Cambs.
Printed by Richard Clay Ltd, Bungay, Suffolk.

Foreword

Contained in this book are the truths and principles God has revealed to me over the last ten years on how to live an over-coming life in Christ Jesus. Walking in daily victory does not have to be a dream but can be a joyful reality.

There are 193 faith-building, how to, inspiring messages that will challenge you to rise up and live a deeper life in Christ as well as give you the tools for overcoming daily.

God has destined us for triumph through the death and resur-rection of his Son Jesus Christ. My prayer is that you will be changed from glory to glory as you read these pages and see the inheritance God has gloriously given to His children.

Dan Chesney

Losing our Marbles

As I was walking up into the mountains to pray one day, I had a marble in my pocket which I had rediscovered when going through several boxes of mementoes. This of course was a special marble because it had survived the years of competition and innumerable moves from one neighbourhood to another.

Now, here I was, a grown man carrying this same marble around again.

I pulled it out of my pocket and ran it through my fingers attempting to recall the feeling of having a winning marble in my hand. It was in excellent condition and, to put it plainly, it was a gem to the little boy inside of me. No wonder I had saved it all these years and still wanted to keep it. Then God said to me, 'Are you still playing with marbles?'

Then, another thought came to me. 'I wonder how many other marbles I'm still carrying around with me?' Jesus said 'For whoever desires to save his life (marbles) will lose it, and whoever will lose his life (marbles) for My sake will find it'. It was then the power of that possessive nature impacted me. I **wanted** to **possess** this marble. It was **mine**, and I had won game after game with it. It was in part representative of **my** status in life.

One of our earliest responses in life is 'to grasp'. And from this first gesture of grasping we never let go. We're always reaching out to possess, to grasp, to take as **our** own. Our pockets get so stuffed with marbles that we're weighed down. Our lives get cluttered and cumbersome.

I knew what I had to do with this prize marble . . . 'let us lay aside every weight, and the sin which so easily ensnares us, and let us run with endurance the race that is set before us'.

I took that marble, which I knew represented many other marbles in my own life and threw it into the bushes. That day I walked down the mountain a little freer, my life a little less cluttered and my heart more deeply implanted in Christ.

Let go of the marbles that may hinder you from achieving God's purpose for you and others. Then, step forward in freedom, with your pockets empty to be filled with God's goodness in the new year.

Mt. 16:25, Heb. 12:1.

Forgetting the Past

Phil. 3:13 'Brethren, I do not count myself to have apprehended; but one thing I do, forgetting those things which are behind and reaching forward to those things which are ahead.'

A lesson every overcomer in Christ must learn is to **forget** the past and keep their eyes on the **goal ahead** of them. If any man had a reason to be bitter, resentful and self-righteous it was Paul. He was criticised, misunderstood, falsely accused, unjustly treated and yet he learned to forget it all and walk in the joy of the Lord.

As Jesus hung upon the cross as a substitute for all our sins, He said 'Father, forgive them, for they do not know what they do.' When Stephen was being stoned by the religious mob he cried out, 'Lord, do not charge them with this sin.' When Paul was on trial at Rome for his faith in Jesus, he said that no one stood with him, everyone deserted him in his hour of need, and yet he writes, 'May it not be charged against them.'

Like Jesus, Christians throughout history have been victorious because they walked in **instant forgiveness**. The sooner you forgive the easier it is to **forget**, the sooner you forgive the less opportunity the hurt has to take root in your heart. The sooner you forgive the quicker you can move ahead.

We go foward by leaving the past behind. Whatever mistakes, sins or unfortunate experiences we have had we leave at the foot of the cross, 'casting our cares upon him.' And then we walk in His resurrection.

When my son was learning to walk he would take a few steps and fall. When he fell he did not remain on the floor saying 'I'll never walk, it's all over.' **No**! He got back up again and took another few steps. Yes, he fell many times but now I am having a hard time keeping up with him.

If you fall, **get up and walk again** and you will find that soon you are running with the best. **Forget those things that are behind and press on for the prize ahead**.

Luke 23:34, Acts 7:60, 2 Tim. 4:16, 1 Peter 5:7.

Shortcomings

Luke 19:3 'And he (Zacchaeus) sought to see who Jesus was but could not because of the crowd, for he was of short stature.'

Zacchaeus was determined to see Jesus. However it was not an easy task because he was short in stature. Being short had probably been a constant source of frustration his whole life. This may have been why he had aspired to be chief tax collector, to compensate for his lack of height.

All of us have some area where we fall short. Repeatedly we may have found like Zacchaeus that it has kept us from seeing Jesus with that clarity we truly desire.

But like Zacchaeus, if we are determined to see Jesus, He will become our shortcomings Compensator. Out of all the crowds, all the needs, all the cheers, requests and shouts, Jesus stopped and recognized Zacchaeus. Oh how this must have made Zacchaeus feel ten feet tall, a giant of a man. Jesus had overcome his shortcomings.

Jesus became the boldness for Peter, the strength for Samson, the husband-Redeemer for Ruth, the courage for Esther. He's the bridge for our sin, the cure for our sicknesses, the supplier for our poverty and our Deliverer in trouble.

Zacchaeus could have allowed his stature to remain an obstacle to him for the rest of his life, but the moment he decided to **see** Jesus, Jesus met him. And once we make that same decision to know Jesus more fully, He will remove all obstacles that dim our vision, and meet us.

Jesus is the Compensator for all shortcomings. Jesus **has already** overcome all obstacles. All that remains is, 'When you seek me with all your heart you shall find me'.

I'm sure when Jesus came to Zacchaeus' house that he forgot all about his lifelong shortcomings, for the great Compensator was **with him**, and so will all your shortcomings fade into the background when you encounter Jesus afresh.

God or Gideon

Judges 6:12–16. And the Angel of the Lord appeared to him, and said to him, 'the Lord is with you, you mighty man of valor!' And Gideon said to Him, 'O my Lord, if the Lord is with us why then has all this happened to us? And where are all His miracles which our fathers told us about, saying, "Did not the Lord bring us up from Egypt?" But now the Lord has forsaken us and delivered us into the hands of the Midianites.' Then the Lord turned to him and said, 'Go in this might of yours, and you shall save Israel from the hand of the Midianites. Have I not sent you?' So he said to Him, 'O my Lord, how can I save Israel? Indeed my clan is weakest in Manasseh, and I am the least in my father's house.' And the Lord said to him, 'Surely I will be with you, and you shall defeat the Midianites as one man'.

Gideon was having a difficult time **believing** the Lord, even though an angelic messenger appeared to him and spoke to him in an audible voice.

In this conversation between the Lord and Gideon we can see two different opinions about the same man. The Lord said Gideon was a **mighty man** with **power** to **defeat** an entire army. Gideon said he was **weak** and insignificant.

If Gideon was going to obey the Lord and succeed in fulfilling God's will, he was going to have to **change** his self-concept, his self-image, his own opinion of himself.

Too often we allow our own opinions and self-concept to doubt God and His word. We judge ourselves by our personal history, what others have told us or by our circumstances. God judges us according to our **heart**. On the inside, in his spirit man Gideon **was** a mighty man, but Gideon wasn't aware of this. He was more aware of his external world, and so he developed a poor self-image.

God is calling us to see ourselves according to His word, according to what He has accomplished in us through Christ. If God says you're **mighty**, you're mighty. If He says you are **righteous**, then you are righteous.

Believe God more than yourself, and like Gideon you too will be able to overcome your foes.

Parable of The Prodigal Son

Read Luke 15: 11–32 Parable of the prodigal son.

The two sons in this parable share a common weakness, they **saw** themselves in relationship to their circumstances. The younger son had left home and because of sin found himself living with pigs, working with pigs, eating what the pigs ate and no doubt smelling like the pigs. In this environment one can imagine he may have felt he was a pig. In this state of mind he says to his father, 'I am no longer worthy to be called your son. Make me like one of your hired servants'.

He now perceived himself as less than he was. He was still a son, but because of his spiritual and physical condition he now saw himself as a servant.

When he came home his father saw his son. He did not accept his son's view but gave him the best robe, a ring and new shoes. The father still treated his son like a son because he **was** a son. Sin had changed his son's perception of himself, but forgiveness brought restoration.

The second son stayed at home and worked among his father's servants. Day after day this son was content to remain at home but he also developed an altered image of himself. He saw himself as just another hired worker on his father's farm. He had worked among the servants so much that he now saw himself as one also.

This image was the reason he never enjoyed his inheritance. He thought he would have to earn his father's inheritance like any servant must earn their wages. He never realized that sons are rightful inheritors just by the simple fact that they are sons.

How many Christians are like these two sons, they have allowed circumstances, sin, religion, working conditions and man's theology to rob them of their inheritance in Christ. Many forget that they are **sons** and so disqualify themselves from the blessings of God.

The devil is out to **steal** our inheritance from us, but if we turn away from sin, Satan's lies, get our eyes off the circumstances and **see Jesus**, who has made us sons and **joint heirs with Him**, then we will live in our inheritance.

Though we fail, He Redeems

Mt. 26:31 Then Jesus said to them, 'All of you will be made to stumble because of me this night, for it is written: I will strike the Shepherd, and the sheep of the flock will be scattered.'

Jesus knew that all His disciples would fail Him in His greatest hour of need, His crucifixion. Jesus knew that all the disciples would sin in that they would forsake Him and deny Him. Yet this foreknowledge did not stop, change or affect the plans Jesus had for His disciples. With all their failings and faults Jesus **still** turned them into the greatest and most effective band of spiritual warriors on the earth on the day of Pentecost. They turned the world upside down in thirty short years.

God knew that Adam and Eve would fail by forsaking **Him** yet He still created them, forgave them, redeemed them and fulfilled His will through them. They were the father and mother of all mankind and from their seed came Jesus Christ.

God knew Samson would fail and bring much hurt to his parents and himself, yet when all looked lost God's perfect will and plan was fulfilled in his death. Samson began to deliver the Israelites from the Philistines.

We have all failed, sinned and even denied our Lord at times, yet he has **not** washed His hands of us. His **grace** is **greater** than our sin. His **redeeming power** overcomes all our failures. His **love forgives** all our denials. All we must do is come back to Him like Adam and Eve, Samson and the disciples did and His glorious purposes **will be fulfilled**.

Nothing, absolutely nothing can stop the redeeming love of God.

If this last six thousand years of history has taught us nothing else, there is this one fact, **love never faileth, love covers a multitude of sins, God's love has overcome the world**, despite all the ravages of time, sin, war, failure, poverty and hurt. God has still **triumphed**!

God is greater than your failure, sin or fear. Turn to Him afresh today and renew the **resurrection of Christ in you!**

My Life

Psalm Forty
O give praise and thanksgiving, for the Lord is mighty,
and His mercy is unending towards His children.
You preserved me in my youth, delivering me from the hand
of the enemy.
You saved me with Your outstretched arm.
I will worship You in Mount Zion.

You anointed me with Your Spirit, filling me to overflowing.
You gave me a new language and songs to sing.
I will rejoice evermore.

You led me through the wilderness as a pilgrim in progress.
Your word was a lamp unto my feet and a light unto my path.
Morning by morning you awakened me and caused my ear to listen.
You taught me Your Name and made me to understand Your Covenant.
I will sing Your praises and clap my hands.

You gave me a wife and children of delight.
You shaped us with love and called us as one.

You led me to the Promised Land.
You gave me eyes to see it from Mount Pisgad.
You gave me grapes to eat.
You anointed me by Your Spirit as I cried with hunger and thirst.
You answered my desire, parted the Jordan and I walked across
on dry land.
You brought me into the Promised Land and satisfied my hungry soul.
I stand in Your mercy with shouts of triumph.

Each day of the battle Your power undergirds.
As Joshua, my Captain, the land we retrieve.
Your arm is not short, Your Word is never failing.
In Christ I am living in union with grace.
I shout on the mountains and dance in the valleys.
Rejoice! Rejoice! For in Him we live and move and have our being.

by D.C.

Wearing whose Costume

Mt 4:3 Now when the tempter came to Him, he said, 'If you are the Son of God, command that these stones become bread.'

When the devil tempted Jesus with food, fame and self-reliance, there was a deeper layer of deception the devil was attempting to perpetrate. It was, 'If you are the Son of God'. In other words Satan was saying '**who do you think you are?**'

Satan's temptation was designed to introduce **doubt** as to **who** Jesus really was, to **doubt** His identity. He does the same with us. The devil wants to blind us to who we are, distort our perception of what we are or fill us with doubt and confusion, creating an identity crisis.

God has created us as **new creatures, righteous** and **His very own children**, but the devil doesn't want us to know or believe it. It's as though he goes around dressing people up in costumes. He tries to dress us up with monkey costumes saying we have come from apes. This is why so many are monkeying around, being mischievous and going bananas. God said we were created in **His image and likeness** which means we're to act like Jesus, not like monkeys.

Some are wearing chicken costumes and they're afraid of everything. They're afraid to witness for Christ, to involve themselves in the work of the ministry. Yet Paul said that as a new creation we do not have the spirit of fear but of **power**, and of **love**, and of a **sound mind**.

Others are wearing bear costumes, roaring, growling and un**bear**able to live with. Can you imagine a chicken and a bear living together as husband and wife. Yet there are many marriages like this.

There are many costumes that Satan has slipped onto God's people, costumes of sickness, depression, anger and discouragement. Others say they're shy, hopeless and unlovable. And because they see themselves wearing these costumes they believe this is **who** or **what** they are. The devil wants us to believe that Christianity is one big costume party, but it's not, it's a **creation party**.

Let's stop all this monkey business and **believe God's word**. We are **blood-washed, made-righteous, healed** and **created in His own image**. We have only **one** costume and that's '**Christ in us**'.

1 Cor. 2:16 Phi.

Christ in You

Col. 1:27 'To them God willed to make known what are the riches of the glory of this mystery among the Gentiles: which is Christ in you, the hope of glory'.

In a hundred different ways the New Testament writers have strained the Greek language under the inspiration of the Holy Spirit to convey to us the glorious meaning of 'Christ in you, the hope of glory'.

Peter writes, 'For you are sons of God now, the live, permanent Word of the Living God has given you his own indestructible heredity.' Paul writes, 'When Christ, who is our life . . .' Christ has, by living in us, become our new life. We share, partake and live in union with His life.

Christ in us is more than just some independent energy source propelling us on. Christ in us is a union of Christ **and** us fulfilling the Father's will by the Holy Spirit.

Christ in us becomes the new us, He is the new man we are instructed to put on. From Genesis to Revelation the Bible has one story after another of people going from self to Christ in them, from the 'old man' to the 'new man'.

The day Moses stood before the burning bush was the day of his transformation. The bush was Moses, the fire was the Holy Spirit and the voice was Jesus, the Living Word. That day Moses-the-bush was purified of sin and self by the sanctifying fire of the Spirit.
Yet the bush remained; as Paul said, 'I am crucified with Christ, nevertheless I live.' Yes, Moses was still there but now instead of Moses proclaiming deliverance to the Israelites it was going to be Christ the Word revealing Himself through Moses the bush. Paul continued, 'Yet **not** I, but Christ liveth in me.' Christ was now living in Moses and rather than Moses going back to Egypt to fail as he did the first time, it was now going to be Christ in Moses going to Egypt to be the Living Word. It was now Jesus Christ *in* Moses, *with* Moses, and *one* in *union* with Moses, which is why he declared in Deuteronomy. 'For He is *your* life, and the length of your days'.

1 Peter 1:23 J.P. Phil., Col. 3:4, Deut. 30:20.

You are Special to God

Acts 10:34 'God is no respecter of persons.'

It was said of Enoch that he 'walked with God'; Of Noah that he 'found grace in the eyes of the Lord.' Abraham was a friend of God. Moses was the humblest man in all the earth; Job was perfect and upright in all his ways. David was a 'man after God's own heart.' Solomon was the wisest man. Daniel was 'greatly beloved'. Peter was called 'the rock', and John was 'the beloved'. Jesus said, 'There had not risen one greater than John the Baptist' and Paul was 'a chosen vessel'.

When we read of people like these we may feel inferior in some way. We may even believe that God loves us less because we have not accomplished or attained all that these great men have. Yet God says He is '**no respecter of persons**', meaning **He** has no favourites, He loves all equally. Though there are specific individuals called for a specific task at a specific time in history, like Esther, a godly woman used as a means to save the Jewish race, this does not mean God thinks less of others.

The Bible says that 'there had not risen one greater than John the Baptist, **but** he who is **least** in the Kingdom of heaven is **greater** than he.' Yes, even the least in God's family are esteemed great in God's eyes. Paul writes 'those members of the body which **seem** to be weaker are **necessary** and those members of the body which we think to be less honourable, on these we bestow **greater honour**, and our unpresentable parts have **greater modesty** but our presentable parts have no need. But God composed the body, having given **greater honour** to that part which **lacks it**'. Do you consider yourself the least, then God has bestowed **greater honour** on **you**.

In God's kingdom we cannot lose, 'for **God so loved the world**,' that includes **all**. The very hairs on our head are known by God; He formed you in the womb; He knows your downsittings and your uprisings. If he causes the sun to shine on the good and evil, surely you are included in His love and grace. Let it be forever known that 'We are a **chosen** generation, a **royal** priesthood, a **holy** nation, His own **special** people.' You are **loved, you** are **special, you** are **important** because **you** are one of His children. 'God is **no** respecter of persons.'

Gen. 5:24, 1 Sam 13:14 KJV, Dan. 10:11, Mt. 11:11, 1 Cor. 12:22–24, John 3:16, 1 Peter 2:9

Following the Vision

Psalm Ten

You are my river of life
   causing me to arise and go forth.
You gave me a vision. I wrote it down;
   it came into my spirit and I rejoiced.

I have made my supplication unto You, O Lord,
   my Strength, my Song, my Hope.
You gave me Your promise and swore by an Oath.
Your Word is forever established.

I am not alone, for I'm planted in Christ,
   my wellspring of life.
I look to no other, but trust in You.
I lean hard upon Your Word and cry out, Abba, Father.
In Christ Alone I stand,
   all other ground is sinking sand.
Amazing grace flows from Your throne.
There's power in the Blood from You Alone.

The vision is now, the task is at hand.
I arise with vigour to see it through.
Upon my knees the battle cry is heard.
With sword in hand, and praise in my mouth
   I take the Promised Land, the vision of God.

You, Alone, have put skill in my hands
   and swiftness in my feet;
to skip over the hill and break through the troops.
The trumpet is sounded. Your voice is heard
   like the sound of mighty waters:
   the enemy is drowned.

Who can stand in the presence of God?
Who can approach His righteous love?
Only those with a contrite spirit,
   whose hearts are sincere and in whom no deceit is found.

In Christ You have made me upright.
I stand in Your joy: deliverance is Your reward . . .
   and peace. My soul's content.
Sing a new song unto the Lord.
His ways are perfect and worthy of all adoration.

(cont.)

He has put within my heart His steps to follow,
to carry out the vision.
His secret in my soul none may see, none may hear . . .
Yet deep has called unto deep
and my soul has followed hard after Thee.

by D.C.

You are Righteous

Rom. 5:19 'For as by one man's disobedience many were made sinners, so also by one Man's obedience many will be made righteous.'

Jesus Christ came to take away our sin and **make us righteous**. This joy is found by all who are washed in the blood of Christ and **know** that **Christ became our sin so we could share his righteousness**.

David was a man who **knew** he was forgiven and that he was righteous in God's sight. He was a man of integrity, godliness and uprightness. He risked his life in fighting Goliath to rescue the Israeli nation, and behaved himself wisely before King Saul.

Yet we find that he was persecuted, hated, envied and despised by Saul. These accusations began to cause David to question his **right-standing** with God, even though he could not personally think of a sin he was committing. He still felt dirty, as though his conscience had been soiled. He asked Jonathan, 'What is my sin before your father?'

How often does this happen to Christians. They step out in faith, they are enjoying this closeness to God, when suddenly they are accused of being wrong.

Jesus received the same treatment, though He was walking in perfect righteousness and obedience to the Father the devil attempted to slow His ministry down by condemning Him, accusing Him, to make Jesus feel He was failing.

This is when we must hold fast our breastplate of righteousness and not allow the enemy to immobilise us by fear of being wrong. Our **righteousness** still stands, and in time God will vindicate us. He exalted David as king proving to all who was right and who was wrong. He resurrected Christ and gave Him the sceptre of righteousness, forever proving that Jesus **is the Truth**. And He will raise you up also.

The tongues may wag and the devil may condemn but God says 'If God be for us who can be against us? **Who** shall lay anything to the charge of God's elect? It is God who justifies, who is he that condemneth?'.

1 Sam. 20:1, Rom. 8:31, 33, 34.

Be Holy

1 Peter 1:16 'Be holy, for I am holy'

Though I had been born-again, baptised in the Holy Spirit and had experienced union with Christ as conqueror, the Risen One, I still wrestled with holiness. I thought that by doing what He asked of me, by walking in obedience to the light I had received that this would put me in a position of both pleasing God and receiving from God.

But one night in prayer I discovered this was not the case. I had failed Him many times and a nagging subconscious condemnation was continually desiring to break through into my conscious mind and truly reveal just how unholy I really was.

In prayer this question of holiness became crystal clear. I saw that my obedience was nothing more than self-effort. That it was 'I' attempting to placate, pacify and please God through works. I had been living under the law.

In the Old Testament holiness was demanded, but the Law made no provision for possibly attaining it. Like the Israelites, I was trying to meet God's condition for receiving His promises by keeping His commandments, yet I never felt I measured up.

But on this night I saw **Christ as my holiness**. Paul wrote, 'It is because of Him that you are in Christ Jesus, who has become for us wisdom from God – that is, **our** righteousness, **holiness** and redemption'.

No longer is it me in my feeble attempt to please God by doing the right thing, but it is now **faith in what Christ is – Holy**. It is **His** holiness that makes me holy and not what I do.

What changed for me? My motive. My good works were a product of fear of failing, or to see what I could receive from Him. It was **self**; but now my motive for living a holy, obedient life is that **I am holy by faith in Christ, the Holy One**. Now I live what I am, rather than living a certain way to become something. I have found His rest. I have ceased from my own efforts to be holy, and have come to rest in faith that **Christ is my holiness**.

The struggle is over, **in Christ** I am holy, unblameable, for Christ has given me **His holiness**.

1 Cor. 1:30 NIV.

Christ as your Life

Phil 1:21 'For to me to live is Christ, and to die is gain'

The ultimate of living is experiencing Christ. Not simply knowing Him, reading His word, or serving Him, but **experiencing His presence**.

Paul said for him to live is Christ, but this is not the case with all people. For some television is their life; for many, success, or sports. For Christians it may consist of services, family or spiritual disciplines. The life however of every Christian is to be, in Christ.

Jacob was a godly man, but he allowed his children to become the centre of his life rather than Jesus. When Joseph (whom Jacob thought was dead) was going to keep Benjamin his brother in Egypt then Judah said to him, 'Now therefore, when I come to your servant my father, and the lad is not with us, **since his life is bound up in the lad's life**, it will happen, when he sees that the lad is not with us, that he will die'.

Benjamin had become the life, the joy, the source of happiness for Jacob, and if anything was to happen to Benjamin, Jacob would die.

But when we come to that place where Paul was, with Christ as his life, then regardless of what happens in life, what is lost, stolen or destroyed, our peace and joy will remain the same because Christ, who is peace and joy **never changes**.

With Christ in us, we can experience Him rather than the world. 1 John 4:18 says that if we're walking in His **love**, we shall not experience **fear**. 1 Peter 1:2 AMP tells us that if we're experiencing Christ's peace, then we shall not feel the agitating passions, fears, frustrations or moral conflicts. Phillipians 4:6–7 says we can have the peace of Christ garrison our hearts and minds so as not to be overcome with anxiety. In Christ we can be more **aware** of His rest than fatigue, of life than death, joy over sorrow and strength more than weakness.

Christ is to be our all-sufficiency. He is our 'all in all', 'you are made complete in Him', 'our life is hid with Christ in God'. And this is exactly what God wants you to be aware of, conscious of and experiencing day by day; Christ our all.

Gen. 44:30–31, Col. 3:11 KJV, Col. 2:10, Col. 3:3 KJV.

I in you and you in Me

John 14:20 'At that day you will know that I am in My Father and you in Me, and I in you'.

One of our great needs is realizing who we are in Christ and who Christ is in us. As Christians we are no longer what the devil says we are. Though he is the accuser of the brethren who constantly tells us of our shortcomings, inadequacies and faults, as well as condemning, blaming, accusing and calling us names. (Now you know the origin of name calling) We, with an understanding of who we are in Christ can expose the devil's whisperings for what they are – lies.

We are no longer what the world says we are. The world is continuously applying peer pressure to make us conform to their ideas. We are told that if we do not dress or speak or conduct ourselves in a certain way then we're not acceptable, good enough or quite up to par. This has made many feel like second rate people. I can remember my father calling me a dummy. He did not mean it with any ill feeling, it was simply a pet name. As a matter of fact (which I came to realize years later) he even used it to express his love. But for me it had a negative effect. I came to believe I was a dummy, and when I brought my grades home from school, I proved I was a dummy.

But in Christ we are now made in His image. Now I have the mind of Christ. I have access to God's divine thoughts. No longer do I see myself as a dummy but as a partaker of the wisdom of Christ. We are what Christ says we are, not what the world or devil say we are. And this liberty comes by staying in God's presence long enough to **know** who you are in Christ and who He is in you.

The 'I CAN' Day

Phil. 4:13 'I can do all things through Christ which strengtheneth me.'

This is your '**I Can**' day in Jesus Christ. Jesus said to His disciples, 'Without Me you can do nothing:'. But Paul now announces that with Jesus Christ we **can do all** things. Solomon wrote that all is vanity and vexations in the earthly life, but he also discovered that with Jesus as his wisdom he could rule the nation of Israel.

In Jesus Christ you can do all things. Moses gave the Lord three excuses why he could not lead the nation of Israel out of Egypt. But the Lord said, 'I will certainly be with you' and in His strength he delivered the three million Jews. Jeremiah told the Lord that he was unable to be a prophet because of his age, but the Lord said to him, 'Do not be afraid of their faces; For I am with you to deliver you.' It was with the Lord that Jeremiah went forth and became a great prophet.

God is not expecting you to become an overcomer without Him. He will not ask or require anything that He is not prepared to help you accomplish. The Lord was the strength for Samson, the wisdom for Solomon, the confidence for Gideon, the beauty for Esther, the grace for Paul, the patience for Job, the miracle-worker for Moses and He is **God** to you also.

Make this confession with me today and then substitute your own words to fit your needs.

I **can** pray through Christ who strengtheneth me.
I **can** love my spouse through Christ who strengtheneth me.
I **can** read the Word through Christ who strengtheneth me.
I **can** overcome through Christ who strengtheneth me.
I **can** prosper through Christ who strengtheneth me.
I **can** walk in health through Christ who strengtheneth me.
I **can** be happy through Christ who strengtheneth me.
I **can** be a witness through Christ who strengtheneth me.

John 15:5, Phil. 4:13, Ex. 3:12, Jer. 1:8.

Living what you Are

Eph. 4:24 '. . . and that you put on the new man which was created according to God, in righteousness and true holiness'.

It is not enough to be a Christian. If we are going to change our world, we must also **live** as a Christian. Once born-again we **are** created in righteousness and holiness. We have God's nature and life. We **are** new creatures in Christ. But now we're to learn how to **live** and **walk** according to what God has created us to be.

This is what Paul means when he says, 'Put on the new man'. The Johnston translation of this verse says, 'Discover new ways of expressing your new, unique personhood in Christ, ways which are in harmony with who you really are . . .' In other words, our spirit man is already created in God's image, but now our outward man needs to **reflect** what God has **already** done on the inside.

Colossians 3:9–10 say, 'Do not lie to one another, since you have put off the old man with his deeds, and have put on the new man who is renewed in knowledge according to the image of Him who created him . . .'. The life aim of a Christian is to learn how to live in harmony with what God has done in us. By the power of the Word and Spirit our outward man begins to be transformed and moulded according to our new self. The Hebrew writer calls this the saving of the soul (Heb. 10:39).

At the present, our spirit man has been made into the likeness of Christ but the soul and body have not. This is why we must clothe ourselves, (our emotion, mind and will), with Christ. We must allow the Word and Spirit to begin bringing it into the likeness of our Christ-like new man.

This is why Paul is constantly saying, 'Clothe yourselves in the new humanity . . .' (Eph 4:24), 'Put off the old man' and 'put on the new man.'

We will only know how to behave or conduct our lives on the outside when we know what He has done on the inside. Fix your eyes on Jesus, in whose image you have been created, for in seeing Him you can see your new self. Then you will know how to live.

Eph. 4:24.

We Have God's Nature

2 Peter 1:4 'There have been given to us exceeding great and precious promises; that through these you may be partakers of the divine nature, having escaped the corruption that is in the world through lust.'

We who are born-again are in union with Christ. We are partakers of His **divine nature**. How magnificent the grace of God is, that we, who were alienated, cut off and without hope, **now** actually share in **God's own life, nature** and **being**.

John 5:26 tells us that 'as the Father has life in Himself, so He has granted the Son to have life in Himself.' Then John 10:10 KJV says 'I (Jesus) come to you that **you** might have life, and life more abundantly.' The **life** in the Father is in the Son and now Jesus **has put that very same life in us**.

It is this God kind of life (Zoe life) that has brought us into union with Christ. That means we share His nature, it means we are family. God's life has become our new nature that we partake of as we believe these exceeding great and precious promises. Listen to how close our relationship with Christ is now because of this work of grace:

'We are bone of His bone, flesh of His flesh.'

'Christ is the head, the church, the body.'

'I am the vine, you are the branches.'

'He who is joined to the Lord is one spirit.'

'We are joint heirs with Christ.'

'For we are **His** offspring.'

'Beloved, now are we the children of God.'

'I in you and you in me.'

'We shall be also in the likeness of His resurrection.'

We're being 'conformed to the image of His Son.'

That we might grow into the 'measure of the stature of the fulness of Christ.

Because we now have God's 'indestructible heredity' we can grow in Christlikeness. We are a **new creature** with **new life** and a **new nature**. Let us forget what we used to be and walk in what we are, **sons** and **daughters of God**.

Eph. 5:31 KJV, Eph. 5:23, John 15:5, 1 Cor. 6:17, Rom. 8:17, Acts 17:28, 1 John 3:2, John 14:20 KJV, Rom. 6:5 KJV, Rom. 8:29, Eph. 4:13, 1 Peter 1:23 J.B.P.

A Song

As snow falling down into the brooks
  blending our differences away, was
As coming to know our Lord Jesus Christ,
  gently carrying me away.

As a mother giving birth unto a child
  blending her pain into love, was
As consummating me into the family;
  prodigal son welcome home.

As a metamorphosis brings new life
  spreading its wings upon flight, was
As I shedding self, accepting new ways,
  consumed by the love of the Lord.

by D.C.

Emancipation Proclamation

Rom. 7:6 'But now we have been delivered from the law, having died to what we were held by, so that we should serve in the newness of the Spirit and not in the oldness of the letter.'

We are **liberated** men and women! We are **free** to follow after Jesus Christ. Our emancipation proclamation has been declared. We 'have been delivered from the powers of darkness and translated into the Kingdom of Jesus Christ'. . . .

We were once slaves to the **law** of sin and death. This law that worked in our flesh was constantly commanding us to serve it. We were captives to the lusts of our flesh, to the dictates of carnality, worldliness and selfishness. We served this law of sin and death by simply doing what it wanted us to do.

But by the glorious work of Calvary, Jesus destroyed, conquered and nullified the power of sin in our lives, thus making us **free** from the law that governs sin. We are no longer slaves to sin but **free** to choose Christ.

Now there is a new law, the law of love, that we are **free** to obey, 'for the law of the Spirit of life in Christ Jesus **has made us free from** the law of sin and death.' Christ is in us by the Holy Spirit, to lead us, teach us and help us become what we were created to be, **children of God**.

As we listen to and obey the Holy Spirit within us, we can walk in God's perfect will. We stay free from sin, death and the devil's deception. Walking in the law of the Spirit of life in Christ Jesus is what now keeps us free from the law of sin and death.

Choose to serve in the newness of the Spirit today. Choose to listen and obey His voice, the prompting and impressions of the Holy Spirit. Choose to be spiritually minded, for this is **how** we walk **not** in the flesh but in the Spirit. As Paul said, we are sons of God because we are being led by the Spirit of God.

Col. 1:13 KJV, Rom. 8:2.

Psalm Of Deliverance from Persecution

Psalm Two

You have heard me, O Lord,
  when I cried out to You in my trouble,
  when my friends persecuted me with
  hurtful sayings and unjust words.
You answered me and lifted me out of my prison.

I was lost and wandering, seeking my way back.
The enemy of my soul whispered lies,
  causing me to stumble into the shadows,
I would have fallen if not for Your Word.
  for my enemies were strong and looking for my downfall,
  but my heart cried out in prayer all the day.
I looked up to see Your hand.

Then came the answer, my fears dissolved,
  the shadows vanished as the entrance
  of Your Word gave light.
I stand as a righteous one,
  clothed in the pure white robe of linen.
You held out to me Your sceptre of righteousness.
My guilt was gone, no more condemned.
The enemy's weapon was broken,
  for the Lord stood by me.

He clothed me in the breastplate of righteousness,
  then into battle we went,
  the accuser could not stand, the persecutor
  had no ground, for the Lord stood by me,
  the Son of Righteousness with healing in His Wings.

My soul has returned to its victory in Christ,
  for all they that put their faith in Him
  shall not be cut off, but the righteous shall
  be in everlasting remembrance.

by D.C.

New Mercies This Day

Lamentations 3:22–23 'Through the Lord's mercies we are not consumed, Because His compassions fail not. They are new every morning; great is His faithfulness.'

This day, **this** day, **this** day are the **mercies** of God new toward you. Not tomorrow, not next week, nor a year from now, but **today**, God's mercy is new. Isaiah tells us that God's mercy is **great** and **sure**; Peter tells us it's **abundant**. David says it is **very great** and plenteous. Paul says He is **rich** in mercy.

There is nothing in your past that can stop God's mercy from reaching you **today**. His mercy endureth **forever**. He shows mercy unto thousands from generation to generation.

Through the sacrificial death and glorious resurrection of His Son Jesus Christ, God has **already** proved to us that He is the 'Father of all mercies'.

Our part is to accept His mercy. Colossians 3:12 says 'Therefore, as the elect of God, holy and beloved, **put on tender mercies** . . .' It is only as we accept God's mercy towards us that we can in turn show mercy to ourselves and to others.

You do not have to go another day living under the hard hand of judgement, criticism and law. God has provided a mercy seat called the Lamb of God. And as we approach the Father through the blood of Christ we are clothed with the same mercy garments Jesus received when He was raised from the dead.

Jesus is God's tender mercy extended towards us. Jesus is God's tender mercy crying 'Father, forgive them, for they do not know what they do.' Jesus is God's tender mercy saying, 'If any man be in Christ, he is a **new** creature, Old things have passed away, Behold all things are become new.' Jesus is God's tender mercy whispering 'I go to prepare a place for **you**'.

This day are His mercies **new**. Look not at the past but only at the cross and know His mercy has **overcome the world**!

New Beginnings

Ps. 118:24 'This is the day which the Lord hath made;
We will rejoice and be glad in it'.

I was facing a difficult situation. I was failing with our second son and the problem was getting worse, not better.

In prayer the Lord gave me the answer to what I was doing wrong, but he also taught me a second lesson. I saw that I did not have to be discouraged or feel sorry for myself even though two years had passed before me, because God is the God of **new beginnings**. Every day is a new start, a new opportunity.

We are not doomed to defeat by our mistakes. Our fate is not sealed by our sins, we have **hope** in Christ who was resurrected from the dead. We can move from failure to success, from defeat to victory, because in Christ 'old things have passed away; **behold**, all things have become new'.

When Peter denied Christ it seemed like he had failed as a friend, a disciple and a minister. Yet Jesus forgave him and empowered him. He then went on to become one of the world's greatest apostles. Paul said 'Forgetting those things which are behind and reaching forward to those things which are ahead . . .'

We have a choice – we can live in the past with all its failings or we can walk with Jesus, our glorious **Redeemer**. Jeremiah said '. . . His compassions fail not. They are **new every morning**; Great is your faithfulness.'

Get God on your side by working with Him, take these four simple steps:

1. *Repent*: Admit your mistakes and failures and then accept your forgiveness.
2. *Be obedient*: **Do** what He tells you to do by the Word and Spirit.
3. *Walk in faith*: Believe God is **now** working out the answer in you and in your situation.
4. *Rejoice Evermore*: See every day as a **new** beginning in Christ where defeat is swallowed up in **victory**!

PRAYER

Dear heavenly Father, I thank you that you are The God of **new beginnings**. I refuse to live in defeat and failure any longer for **You** are my **hope** and **salvation**. Forgive me for my sins, blindness and disobedience. Step into my life and this problem, with Your grace and power and become my **new beginning**. I will walk by faith knowing You are my answer and **rejoice evermore** as I am no longer alone.

2 Cor. 5:17, Phil. 3:13, Lam. 3:22–23.

The Lamb taketh Away

John 1:29 '. . . Behold! The Lamb of God who takes away the sins of the world!'

The most magnificent redemptive fact of the gospel is that Jesus takes away sin. He has **blotted** out our sin (Is. 44:22). He **remembers** it **no more** (Is. 43:25). He has **cast all** our sins **behind** His back (Is. 38:17). He has **destroyed** the **yoke** of sin by the anointing (Is. 10:27). He has made our crimson sins as **white as snow** (Is. 1:18). He has **trodden** our sins **beneath his feet** and **thrown** them into the **depths** of the ocean (Micah 7:19). He has **pardoned, forgiven** and **healed** us of our sin. He has **put away** sin by the sacrifice of Himself (Heb. 9:26) and Jesus has **purged** us of our sins.

God has completely, thoroughly, absolutely and unequivocably taken our sins away by the death and resurrection of Jesus Christ our Saviour.

Never again do we have to live under the shadow of our past when we now live under the blood of Jesus our Righteousness. So clean and pure have our hearts been made that now the New Testament writers dare to write: And you, who once were alienated and enemies in your mind by wicked works, yet **now** He has **reconciled** in the body of His flesh through death, to present you **holy** and **blameless** and **irreproachable** in His sight, if indeed you continue in the faith . . .' And again 'Now unto Him that is able to keep you from falling, and to present you **faultless** before the presence of His glory with exceeding joy'. And still further they say 'Whereby He is able also to save them to the uttermost . . .'

What sin, what fault, what mistake, what evil cannot be conquered by the blood of Christ? If you are a child of God they have **all been taken away by the Lamb of God**.

We have only one song to sing for all eternity:-
Worthy is the Lamb who was slain
And has redeemed us to God by His blood.

Col. 1:21–23, Jude 29, Heb. 7:25, Rev. 5:12,9.

Praise belongs to the Lord

Psalm Three

O people, let the praises roar with thunder!
Blow the mighty trumpets and sound the loud cymbals.
Clap your hands all you saints,
shout with the voice of trumpets,
For the enemy shall flee.
He shall see your praise, and fear,
for the church has clothed herself in
The garment of praise
and has entered into the chamber
of her beloved.
They are behind the door,
safe in the arms of love.
The Lord, He is one with His Bride.

O give praise unto the Lord all you people
O give thanksgiving for His Name is Great
Worship the beauty of His Holiness
And leap upon the hills all you that are called.

You have put praises in my heart,
How can I not but sing them?
You are my joy and delight,
my sunshine and morning light.

How can I be quiet when all earth
is full of Your glory
And Your people You preserved?

In praise Your people return to their rest.
In praise Your people do love You.
O sing of His mercy, for He is gracious
unto the poor and needy,
He lifts them up and fills them with good things.
He is righteous in all His ways,
full of compassion and tender care.

Burst into song, let His praises ring
for the Lord has heard us, He is on our side.
He has not left His people alone, He is by
their side, answering them when they cry.

(cont.)

I will take great delight in You, O God,
And I will bless Your holy, wonderful Name,
that is above all other names.
My song will be unto You
for You art worthy to receive praise and glory.

You led Israel out of the fiery furnace.
You have delivered me from my destruction.
You, alone, have redeemed mankind.

Let all the angels sound the trumpets:
Bring forth the music of heaven.
Let all nature give her praise,
and Zion her worship,
for You dwell in Judah.
Be glad in the praises of Your children.

You made Judah Your sanctuary and You sent
it forth in front of the battle
Therefore I will give You praise,
for the battle is the Lord's.
He is my strength and shield, my defence
and fortress.

A well-spring of praise flows up
from the depths of my soul,
ever refreshing like a river.
Your praise flows up to You,
gathering into Your heart, O Lord.

You are marvellous in praise, wondrous to behold.
Let all the earth break forth and rejoice
for You are established on Your throne.

The heaven of heavens cannot contain You,
And the works of men cannot build You
a dwelling place,
But You inhabit the praises of Your people.

by D.C.

Forgiveness

Eph. 4:32 'Be kind to one another, tenderhearted, forgiving one another, just as God in Christ also forgave you'.

The greatest attribute and expression of love is forgiveness. Jesus not only forsook all when leaving heaven to come to earth, but He endured the depths of human and demonic cruelty on the cross. In the midst of His agony, with His body broken, His heart bleeding and His spirit blackened by the sin of man's rebellion, He cries out, 'Father **forgive** them, for they do not know what they do'.

The loving heart of Jesus can be also seen in Moses, a man who sacrificed all. He left Egypt, giving up his career, wealth, authority, position and prestige. He isolated himself for 40 years to find God's will and way. And then after going back to Egypt and bringing deliverance to the Israelites, they were ungrateful, slanderous and rebellious. They blamed Moses for their troubles, attempted insurrection and even wanted to stone him. Yet in prayer, the heart of Christ is spoken through Moses as he says, 'Yet now, if You will **forgive** their sin – but if not, I pray, **blot me out** of Your book which you have written'.

Paul had this same heart. His greatest desire was to see the Jewish people find their true Messiah, Jesus Christ. To this Paul gave his life, sacrificing everything, expending every resource and talent he had. But many Jews hated him even as they did Christ. They rejected him, beat him, stoned and imprisoned him. They robbed him, ran him out of town and city. They accused, mocked and slandered him. And yet like Moses his prayer for his enemies was, 'I wish that **I myself were accursed from Christ** for my brethren, my kinsmen according to the flesh'.

So constraining and all consuming was the love of God in the heart of Moses and Paul that they were willing to forfeit their salvation in Christ (the most precious gift of time immortal) to see others find Christ.

Moses and Paul did not have to make that sacrifice, Christ made it for them, and for us. God **forgave** us because Jesus was willing to become our sin, to die our death, and be separated from the Father and thereby bring us **forgiveness**.

Can you not hear the Spirit saying to you today, 'and be kind to one another, tenderhearted, **forgiving one another just as God** in Christ also **forgave** you'.

Luke 23:34, Ex. 32:32, Rom. 9:3 KJV.

The Man of the Gadarenes

Mk 5:5 'And always, night and day, he was in the mountains and in the tombs, crying out and cutting himself with stones'.

Walking in victory on a daily basis seems nearly impossible for those who have had the stones of life thrown at them, cutting deeply into their heart and soul. Crying may be more of a way of life than 'rejoicing evermore'.

Elijah challenged the prophets of Baal on mount Carmel to see who was the Living God, the God who would answer by fire. The prophets of Baal began to pray, to call out to their god. When no response came they started dancing, cutting themselves with stones and crying out. And still there was no response. Only after many hours did they give up exhausted, desolate and broken, knowing their god did not understand their cry, nor did he come to heal their cuts.

The man of the Gadarenes was up in a mountain all alone, cutting himself also. Day and night he cried out but there was none to help him either. Like the prophets of Baal his cry was in vain and his cuts were terminal.

But this is not so for the Christian, we have a Saviour who is easily touched with our cuts and cries. For we have a Saviour who came down and bore **our** cuts and tears.

See this man Jesus who bore **our griefs** and **sorrows**. He was **stricken, smitten** by God and **afflicted**. He was **wounded** and **bruised**, suffered our **chastisement** and **by his stripes** we are healed. On Jesus was **laid** our iniquity. He was **oppressed, slaughtered** like a Lamb. He was taken to **prison, cut off** from the living. He was **violently** treated, **died** and went down into the **grave**. His soul was made an **offering** for sin. Yes, Jesus was **poured** out, **marred**, and **numbered** with the criminals.

Jesus has experienced all our **cuts** and **tears**, but even **more** than that, **He has overcome them all**. **He** arose from the dead a Conqueror over tears, hurts, stones, cuts, shame, loneliness, misunderstandings and **everything** that touches the heart of man to destroy it. The Man of Gethsemane is the same Man of Victory.

Give Him your cuts, your tears and your hurts for He has overcome them all by His love and sacrifice. **He understands you.**

A Clear Conscience

1 Cor. 4:4 NEB 'I have nothing on my conscience'.

What a daring statement for Paul to make, 'I know **nothing** against myself.' Most people never feel quite good enough. They always think they are lacking something. In the back of their minds there is this gnawing that in some way there is sin in their lives. For many, condemnation is something that is continually waiting for them around every corner.

Yet Paul found the secret of living at peace with himself and God. He could boldly say, 'I have nothing on my conscience.' When Paul was standing before the Sanhedrin and being accused of breaking the law and defiling the temple, he was able to say, 'I have lived in all good conscience before God until this day.' When writing to Timothy he again said, 'I thank God, whom I serve with a **pure** conscience . . .'

Paul had overcome those nagging accusing thoughts and feelings of never measuring up, because he discovered, 'There is now no condemnation to those who are **in Christ**.' Being **in Christ** means that through the blood of Christ our **conscience has been purged** from dead works to serve the Living God, **our hearts have been sprinkled from an evil conscience**.

This means that whatever sin we committed before salvation it is completely and totally and absolutely forgiven. We **never** have to compare ourselves with what we were. But this cleansing and purging process does not end there, the blood of Christ is ever efficacious. 1 John 1:9 says 'If we confess our sins, He is **faithful** and **just** to **forgive us** our sins and to **cleanse us** from **all** unrighteousness. Our conscience can remain pure and clean for our whole life. Like Paul we can '**overcome** him (the devil) by the **blood** of the **Lamb** . . .' **We have been justified by His precious blood.**

That's why Paul could stand before his accusers and say, 'I have lived in all good conscience before God until this day.' Had Paul never made a mistake or sinned? No! But like you and me he **knew** he had been **forgiven and cleansed by the blood of Jesus**.

Acts 23:1, 2 Tim. 1:3, Rom. 8:1, Heb. 9:14, 10:33, Rev. 12:11, Rom. 5:9.

Love on a Cross

They stood all around
  while love hung on a cross.
They shouted and jeered,
  they cajoled and reared.
Yet love remained fastened,
  held by eternal cords.
No one could see the Father's grace,
  for Christ was covered with sin's evil face.
Then love breathed its last,
  it sighed, it bowed its head.
The moon covered its face,
  the sun gave no light.
The earth quaked in terror,
  and the angel sang no song.
Blinded were the masses to love's giving way,
  for this was the hour when wickedness swayed.
Then up from the grave, out of hell itself,
  came love's unfailing power,
  triumphing through sacrifice.
The cry came from heaven,
  God had purged humanities leaven.
The sceptre had been extended
  and righteousness given.
Love's sweet incense has risen
  and death has lost its sting.
Mankind's soul now liberated by love,
  anointed and blessed by the Holy Dove.

by D.C.

Love is Unconquerable

John 3:16 'For God so loved the world that He gave His only begotten Son, that whoever believes in Him should not perish but have everlasting life'.

Love is why Jesus was unconquerable. They threatened His reputation, His friends, His future and His life in order to persuade Him to compromise, but Jesus remained unchanged. Love was willing to be crucified so He had no fear of death. Love was willing to lose all, which is why He feared no loss. Christ gave **all** so none could take from Him.

And this is the love that makes us conquerers also. John wrote, 'And they **overcame** him by the blood of the Lamb and by the word of their testimony, **and they did not love their lives to the death**'. Like Christ, once we have given all, then we lose all fear of loss. Now the devil and man have nothing to threaten or bribe us with.

It was **love** that sang when Paul and Silas were in prison with bleeding backs. It was **love** that prayed when Daniel was informed that prayer was outlawed. It was **love** that changed Stephen's face to the likeness of an angel in the midst of his persecutions. And it is **love** that will enable **you** to **follow Jesus** whatever the cost.

We can speak in other tongues, intercede in fifteen different languages, have a conversation with Gabriel and speak as an oracle of God, but if we have not love we shall be overcome by criticism and contrary opinions.

Love is so unparalleled that even if we could prophesy the future, teach with authority and revelation knowledge, have faith to part the Red Sea, to remove any mountain, to give all our prosperity to the poor, we would still fall short because without **love** we are **nothing**. In other words, without **love** we could **not** be conquerers, overcomers, victorious Christians.

Love never fails because it suffers long, endures all things, believes all things and always puts others first. Love will die to see another raised up. Love will give to see another have, Love will forfeit to have another benefit. Love will weep to see another laugh. Love will go to battle to set another free. Love will humble itself to see another exalted.

Fear will bring us defeat but **love** will bring us victory. How? By letting go of everything that we would fear to lose and placing our lives in God's Almighty hands. Jesus did this when He said:
'Into thy hands I commit my spirit'
and God raised Him from the dead!
Love never fails

Rev. 12:11, Luke 23:46 KJV, 1 Cor. 13:8.

Love your Enemies

Mt. 5:44 'But I say to you, love your enemies, bless those who curse you, do good to those who hate you, and pray for those who spitefully use you and persecute you'.

Jesus gives us four ways to overcome evil in this verse. To love our enemies, bless people who curse us, be helpful to those who hate us and finally, to pray for people who take advantage of us and even ridicule us. Paul reiterated this truth in Romans 12:20–21: 'Therefore if your enemy hungers, feed him; If he thirsts, give him a drink; for in so doing you will heap coals of fire on his head. Do not be overcome by evil, but overcome evil with good.'

This is the pathway of God's love, a love that never fails. Jesus, our supreme example overcame **all** evil by His willing crucifixion at the hands of wicked man. Out of the extremity of cruelties came the pinnacle of triumph. The enemies were overthrown and curses swallowed up. The hateful were stunned and ridiculers silenced. Christ's simple prayer on the cross, 'Father forgive them, for they know not what they do,' overcame the gates of hell.

This truth was forcefully brought home to me one day when working as a cook in a restaurant; I was responsible for all kitchen employees and a new employee had just been hired. Trouble started immediately with this young man, until one day he arrogantly refused to finish his work and walked off. I remember walking home that day seething with anger. In my mind I was planning his 'unemployment' at the restaurant. When I arrived at home I fell on my knees and poured out my desire for God's way. In a moment the answer came, 'Do good to those who hate you, and pray for those who spitefully use you . . .'. Joy flooded my heart, I had heard from heaven, I had found God's way. My anger was gone, my thoughts were changed, I only wanted to ask this person to forgive me for my anger.

The following day I approached him and to his astonishment I asked him to forgive me. His heart was melted and he in turn asked the same of me.

The young man was still an unprofitable employee but God had removed the problem from my heart and hands. In two days the manager gave him his 'walking papers', removing the source of the problem, while God had removed the bitterness from my heart. God's way had overcome the wrong and peace reigned.

Luke 23:34, Mt. 5:49.

Our son Joshua's
1st Psalm at age Four Aug. 2 1985

Psalm Thirty Six
God, He is Lord
He loves you
He doesn't want you to do any **No No's**
Only He can forgive you by dying on the Cross.

Love Casts Out Fear

1 John 4:18 'There is not fear in love; but perfect love casts out fear.'

One day as Jesus was teaching the people, the Scribes and Pharisees brought a woman to Him who they had caught in adultery. As she stood there in the midst of the crowd the Pharisees said to Jesus, 'Teacher, this woman was caught in adultery, in the very act. Now Moses in the law, commanded us that such should be stoned. But what do you say?'

How fear must have gripped this woman's heart when she heard the words 'be stoned'. Her whole life was in the balance as the fear of death hung over her head. Everybody's eyes as well as hers were on Jesus. Would His words bring life, or would they bring death?

Then Jesus arose and said 'He who is without sin among you, let him throw the first stone.' And when the angry crowd heard this they were convicted by their consciences and left one by one until there was no one left but Jesus and the woman.

Silence filled the air. Could she dare believe she was free? Then Jesus said to her, 'Woman, where are your accusers? Has no one condemned you?' She said, 'No one, Lord.' And Jesus said to her, 'Neither do I condemn you; go and sin no more.'

That day perfect love **cast out** fear. And that same love is 'being shed abroad in our hearts.' Jesus has not come to condemn but to **save** us. **He** did not come to punish but to **pardon** us. **He** did not come to accuse but to **justify** us.

Like this woman Jesus came to release us from the fear of death, the fear of shame, the fear of people. As His children He has not given us a spirit of fear but rather a spirit of love. God's love suffers long and is kind, it is not envious, proud or arrogant. It doesn't seek its own advantage and thinks **no** evil.

It doesn't laugh when we fail but rather rejoices when we succeed. It bears **all** things, believes **all** things, hopes **all** things, endures **all** things. Love **never** fails, it **will conquer** every fear we may experience.

John 8:4–5, 7, 10–11.

Love Conquers

1 John 4:16 'And we have known and believed the love that God hath to us. **God is love**; and he that dwelleth in love dwelleth in God, and God in him.'

There is an eternal fact that will forever change your life, and that is: **God is love**. So far reaching, so comprehensive, so all encompassing is this truth that God in Christ conquered all sin, sickness, the devil and death by **love**'s work on the cross. 'In this is love, not that we loved God, but that He loved us, and sent His Son to be the propitiation for our sins.'

All we must do now is accept and walk in His love, and as we do we also are **more** than conquerors. Paul declared '. . . in **all** these things we are **more** than **conquerors** through him that **loved** us.' What things? All things listed in Romans 8:35; 'unwarranted charges, condemnation, tribulation, distress, persecution, famine, nakedness, peril or war. Not death or life, angels or principalities, powers or things present, not the future. Not even events in the heavens or on the earth. Not any creature can separate us from the **love of Christ in God**.'

John tells us 'perfect love casts out fear . . .' as well as guilt and shame. Solomon says, 'Love covers all sins.' Love is what has conquered all.

This **love, God's love** is your answer to all of life's problems. For **God so loved** the world that He **gave** . . .'. His love was sent to **save you, help you, deliver you**. **God** sent Jesus to **bless you** (Acts 3:26). David shouted 'This I know, because God is for me.' James said 'Every good gift and every perfect gift is . . . from the Father above.'

The essence of God is **love**, the essence of **love** is giving and the essence of **giving** is sacrifice. All three are seen in Jesus and what He has done for us. And because of the cross He has forever proved **love never fails**. That's why you are **more** than a **conqueror**, because in His **love you cannot fail either**.

1 John 4:10, Rom. 8:35–39 L.B., 1 John 4:18, Pr. 10:12, John 3:16, Ps. 56:9, James 1:17 KJV.

Eyes of Love

1 John 4:11 'Beloved, if God so loved us, we also ought to love one another.'

One evening as my wife and I were talking she turned to me and said 'Honey, I love everything about you'. I was shocked. How could my wife love **everything** about me knowing more about me than any other person? I then asked her, 'How can you love me in such a way?' She answered, 'Because I see you through eyes of love.' It wasn't until a year later that I was able to say the same thing to her.

What liberty the love of Christ has brought into our home. We don't have to hide or pretend to be something we are not. We are not only 'accepted into the beloved' but we are accepted by each other. It has brought joy into our marriage.

John wrote that 'perfect love (God's kind of love) casteth out fear'. My wife and I are not afraid of our weaknesses or faults being exposed because we know we are loved and that this love will not discontinue or be withheld at certain moments. Rather, Christ-like love in us will suffer long if need be, it will remain kind and will not think evil. This love will bear all, make us continue to believe in each other and will hope for the best. It will endure to the end because the love God has given us is found in Christ, not in each other. He has become the stability and cornerstone of our marriage.

Our desire to please each other is a result of our love, not of our fear that we will no longer be acceptable. As we look back at this miracle of grace God has given to us, we can see that love is the creative desire for maximizing all the potential good within ourselves for each other and for Christ. Jesus has done what we could not, giving us peace with ourselves, each other and with God.

We can say through daily sharing of life that 'love never fails'. It has conquered the temper, impatience, broken dreams and the wild beasts of selfishness and self importance.

'In this the love of God was manifested toward us, that God has sent His only begotten Son into the world that we might **live through Him**.'

Eph. 1:6, 1 John 4:18 KJV, 1 Cor. 13:8, 1 John 4:9.

Prayer

Holy Father, Righteous God!
How we rejoice to call You Father,
We can stand before You,
  in the righteousness of Christ;
  without shame, guilt or inferiority.

Our hearts leap
  when we think of Your acceptance of us.
For You have made us
  accepted in The Beloved.

How Your grace flows from Your heart.
Christ Jesus, we call You Master,
  Saviour, Holy and Pure.
We yield and submit, surrender and
  give ourselves up to You by the Spirit.

We are filled with thanksgiving, because
  we are partakers of Your Divine Nature.
We can sense, feel and know Your Glory.

by D.C.

Jesus made the Way

Heb. 5:16 'Let us therefore come boldly to the throne of grace, that we may obtain mercy and find grace to help in time of need'.

Surely God has given us unshakeable grounds for believing that we can come before His throne, enter into His presence and obtain the answer to our prayers.

Jesus, having obtained eternal redemption for us, has made the way. We can now come **boldly** in the name of Jesus, by the blood of Jesus, because we are heirs with Christ Jesus to all the Father has, because Jesus ever lives to make intercession for us, because we have been sanctified, cleansed, and purged of sin and dead works.

We can now approach the Father because Jesus our Mediator has given us a better covenant with better promises. We can enter the throneroom because we're family, sons and daughters of God. We have been justified, acquitted, forgiven, called, predestined, glorified, redeemed, accepted, adopted, and born of God. We are part of the Seed of Christ, engrafted into the Vine, circumcised of the flesh and made heirs to the promises of God.

We are now under grace, recipients of His mercy and objects of His love, and reconciled. We are called saints, the bride of Christ, believers, the temple of God, and the body of Christ.

What more could God do or say to reveal to us that we are welcomed into His throne of grace? Clearly He is saying, 'Your answers are waiting for you'.

Jesus has brought us near to the Father. He has made peace between us and Him. Now as Paul says, 'For through Him we have access by one Spirit to the Father. **Now**, therefore, you are no longer strangers and foreigners, but fellow citizens with the saints and members of the household of God . . .'.

God answered our prayer and met our need when we were sinners. **How much more** is His **abundant heart prepared to give to us now**.

And Jesus said to the leper, 'I am willing be cleansed.'

Eph. 2:18–19, Mk. 1:41.

Jesus Our Forerunner

Heb. 6:20 'Where the forerunner has entered for us, even Jesus, having become High Priest forever according to the order of Melchizedek.'

How many of us constantly endeavour to receive from God by works. We put our faith in how much we pray, read the word or attend church.

This kind of thinking is all on self which is exactly why we don't receive. It is not a matter of what we do or don't do, but rather what **Jesus did** and **is**.

Our faith is to be only in the finished atoning work of Jesus Christ. Jesus, after His death, resurrection and ascent, **entered into the throne room** and **obtained everything from the Father for us**. Jesus has gone on **before** us to secure 'every spiritual blessing in heavenly places'.

This means that whatever we need, desire or are seeking for, Jesus has **already** secured it. And this is why our faith is in Jesus and not in what we do.

Our boldness to approach the Father in prayer comes by the blood of Jesus, who has made a new and living way for us to enter the Holiest place of all.

We do not have to **be** somebody, or have gone through any particular life experience to receive from God. God didn't choose Israel to inherit the promised land because of their deep spiritual life. God didn't choose Esther for her courage and brave deeds and He hasn't chosen us because of our human assets either. Paul tells us in 1 Cor. 1:26–27, 'For you see your calling, brethren, that not many wise according to the flesh, not many mighty, nor many noble, are called. But God has chosen the foolish things of the world to put to shame the wise; but God has chosen the weak things of the world to put to shame the things which are mighty.' Why? **'That no flesh should glory in His presence.'**

All that is ever done, all that is good, all that is accomplished in building God's Kingdom **is because of Jesus' blood and righteousness.**

Receive by faith today, turn aside from works and rest in Christ, for everything we're ever to receive has already been secured by Christ our forerunner.

Eph. 1:3 KJV.

Jesus Praying through Us

John 11:22 'But even now I know that whatever You ask of God, God will give You'.

Martha said this to Jesus because she had faith in His prayers. She knew that if **Jesus asked** the Father, He would grant the request to Him, **whatever** it was.

Now listen to what Paul says to us in Romans 8:26, 'Likewise the Spirit also helps in our weaknesses. For we do not know what we should pray for as we might, but the **Spirit Himself makes intercession for us** with groanings which cannot be uttered'. Here Martha's words are being fulfilled, Jesus is **now** praying in and through us **by the Holy Spirit**.

This is the kind of prayer life God is calling us to, because when Jesus by the Holy Spirit is praying through us, then **whatever He is asking the Father will answer**.

Ask yourself this question: What is Jesus praying through you by the Spirit? What has He filled your heart with? Whatever it is, we can say with absolute confidence and joy that the Father is going to grant it.

Jesus turned to Martha and said, 'Did I not say to you that if you would believe you would see the glory of God? What is the glory we will see? The **answer** to our prayer. For Martha it was the resurrection of Lazarus but for us it will be for what we are praying, whether big or small. Any answer from God is a visible manifestation of God in our prayer life. That is the glory, that is God.

Jesus Himself said, 'Father, I thank You that You have heard Me. And I know that You **always** hear Me . . .' Jesus **knows** the Father **always** hears Him, which is why He is ever interceding (through us) at the right hand of the Father. And since we **know** that it is Christ in us by the Holy Spirit praying, then we can also **know** that the **Father hears us**. And to this John writes in 1 John 5:15 'And if we **know** that He hears us, **whatever we ask, we know that we have the petitions** that we have asked of Him.'

Can you not hear Jesus saying to you right at this moment 'that if you would believe you would **see** the glory of God?'

John 11:40, John 11:41–42.

Spending Time at the Top

Ps. 18:33 'He makes my feet like the feet of deer, and sits me on my high places.'

God's will, desire and plan for us is to make us the **head** and **not** the tail, to be **above** and **not** beneath. To be successful and **not** a failure. The pathway of a Christian is **heaven** bound, **upward** bound, **glory** bound. There will be no failures or losers in heaven.

Jesus was successful. He accomplished exactly what He set out to do, which was to deliver us from the powers of hell. He fulfilled His goal while on earth and we can say He has made it to the top. His Name is above every other name, His position above every position. He has all power and authority in heaven, in earth and even under the earth. He is seated at the right hand of God the Father '**far above all** principalities and power and might and dominion.' Now that's going places!

And the Bible goes on to say that if we will join God's family then He'll do in us what He did in Jesus His Son. He'll '**raise** us **up** and make us to sit in **heavenly places** in **Christ Jesus**'. We can ride on the success of Jesus, we can follow in His footsteps right to the top also. God did not save us to be two time losers but rather to **reign** in righteousness with Christ Jesus our Lord.

However, there is something we must do, and that is, spend time at the top. Paul says in 1 Cor. 15:33 (AB) 'Evil companionship corrupts good morals and character.' In other words, who you spend time with determines your destiny.

When the Pharisees saw the successful ministry of the disciples they could only come to one conclusion, 'they (the disciples) had been **with Jesus**'. Success comes by being with success, losing comes by being with losers. Spend time at the top with Jesus, leaving the carnal behind and you will soon find that promotion comes from God.

Eph. 1:22, Eph. 2:6, Acts 4:13.

Intercession precedes Possession

Matthew 11:12 'And from the days of John the Baptist until now the Kingdom of Heaven suffers violence, and the violent take it by force'.

Intercession is like stepping into a Roman coliseum to do battle with the lions, gladiators and warriors of hell. It's a spiritual activity that often demands violent action in order to recapture ground that was illegally possessed by Satan.

Paul said, 'For we do not wrestle against flesh and blood, but against principalities, against powers, against the rulers of the darkness of this age, against spiritual hosts of wickedness in the heavenly places'.

Wrestling is a **contact** sport, you are face to face with your opponent who is breathing down your neck. Spiritual warfare also means contact, it's your spirit battling with an evil spirit. It involves binding, casting out, resisting, putting to flight the forces of darkness, and planting the banner of Christ on the newly gained territory.

Joshua and the Israelites taking possession of the promised land is a vivid example of this. He was told that wherever he would **tread**, that portion of land would be his. In other words, it was going to take violent, aggressive action, **treading** in order to possess the land. In the New Testament treading is likened to prayer. **First** we take it in prayer (in the spirit realm) then we possess it in the natural realm.

It is **not** that we are violently rushing the throne of God but rather we are violently praying for the removal of satanic powers between earth and heaven. God has already said **yes** to His will, but we do have an enemy who is constantly saying **no**. This is why **intercession precedes possession**. Jesus conquered Calvary in the garden of intercession, His crucifixion, death and resurrection were the out-living of His prayer victory.

Do you long for more victories in your life? Then do battle on your knees. Take possession in prayer and then walk in obedience to the answers.

Eph. 6:12.

The Violent take it by Force

Matthew 11:12. 'And from the days of John the Baptist until now the Kingdom of heaven suffers violence, and the violent take it by force.'

Taking the kingdom of heaven by violent force is doing what the nation of Israel did when they possessed the promised land of Canaan. The Lord said to Joshua, 'Every place that the sole of your feet will tread upon I have given you, as I said to Moses.'

As far as God was concerned the land was theirs, but they were going to have to **enter** the land, **conquer** the land, **settle** the land. Once **they** had placed their feet upon the land, **trodden** down and **subdued** their enemies, then they could enjoy it.

Today we have inherited a promised land also, our inheritance in Christ. Paul wrote, 'Blessed be the God and Father of our Lord Jesus Christ who has blessed us with **all** spiritual blessings in heavenly places in Christ.' Peter writes 'According as His divine power hath given unto us **all** things that pertain unto life and godliness, through the knowledge of him that hath called us to glory and virtue.' 2 Corinthians 1:28 KJV says, '**For all** the promises of God in him are yea, and in him Amen, unto the glory of God **by us**.'

Now we stand at the river Jordan with the promised land before us and God is saying, 'The land is yours, go in and possess it.' How do we tread and conquer? By prayer! Not only shall we have to ask and seek but sometimes we have to knock **until** the door is opened.

The devil is out to steal, kill and destroy and it will take the violent force of the Holy Spirit to wrestle his agents to the ground and pin them down. We must raise the Sword of the Spirit, the Word of God and persevere in prayer until the battle is over. Paul said, 'Be strong in the might and power of the Lord.' Jude said, 'Contend for the faith.' Peter said 'Be sober, be vigilant . . . resist him (the devil) steadfast in the faith.'

Like Caleb we can say 'Let us go in for we are well able to take the land.' And we can take it because He said, 'And the violent **take it by force**' – the force of prayer energised by God.

Josh. 1:3, Eph. 1:3 KJV, 2 Peter 1:3 KJV, 1 Peter 5:8–9, Num. 13:30 KJV.

Asking

James 4:2 'Ye have not because Ye ask not'.

Asking is fundamental to prayer and is a privilege given to every child of God. Within one conversation, Jesus reminds, instructs and even commands His disciples 7 times to **ask** in prayer. James tells us we have not because we **ask** not. The Lord said to Isaiah 'Ask Me of things to come concerning My sons . . .' In Psalm 2:8 we read of the Father saying to Jesus 'Ask of Me and I will give you the nations for your inheritance, and the ends of the earth for your possession'.

Our salvation was contingent upon Jesus asking the Father for you and for me. We are part of the nations He asked for when He prayed while on earth. So important is asking that every intervention of God into mankind's history was as a result of somebody **asking**.

Lot was saved from destruction because Abraham **asked**. The disciples received the Holy Spirit because they **asked**. You were saved because somebody **asked**. Even though the promises have been given, we must still '**ask**, and it shall be given'.

The world, the flesh and the devil will give you reason upon reason why you should not ask, but **God is saying ask**! Come to the Father with a new confidence, that the reason He wants you to ask is so He can **answer, give** and **share** with you His glorious riches.

When Jesus was suffering for our sins on the cross, He still did not refuse the penitent thief when he **asked** for forgiveness. Jesus immediately **answered**. And why? Because the reason Jesus died was to **remove all hindrance that would keep us from asking**. He is saying to you today:

'*Let us* **therefore** come boldly to the throne of grace, that we may obtain mercy and find grace to help in time of need'.

Ask!

Is. 45:11, Mt. 7:7, Heb. 4:16.

What you Pray makes a Difference

Reading: Genesis 18:17–33

When the Lord was standing before Abraham He said, 'Because the **outcry against** Sodom and Gomorrah is great, and because their sin is very grievous, I will go down now and see whether they have done altogether according to the **outcry against it** that has **come to me** . . .' Evidently somebody was telling God in prayer of the corruption and wickedness. They were crying out to God for something to be done about the situation. And because of this person's prayer, judgement was about to be executed.

But God's desire is **always to save**, which is why He was sharing with Abraham the pending destruction of Sodom and Gomorrah. He was looking for an intercessor, one who would ask for mercy, forgiveness and salvation. God was on His way to answer the prayer of the one crying out for judgement because He is a God of justice and judgement. But He is also a God of love and mercy, so He needed someone to **ask** in prayer for mercy.

Abraham responded to God's heart and began to intercede. First he asked God to spare the cities for 50 righteous people, but then, realising how willing God was to forgive and show mercy, he eventually agreed that for 10 righteous people God would spare the cities.

I believe if Abraham had continued to intercede, God would have spared the cities for 1 righteous person. This shows us the power of prayer and the mercy of God. Yet God's mercy did make up for Abraham's short-sighted intercession. Not even 10 righteous people could be found. Lot's family alone was at least 8, and probably 10, which is why Abraham may have settled for that figure. But only 4 of them were found worthy to escape. So God took Abraham's prayer, added His blessed mercy to it, and spared Lot, his 2 daughters and Zoar, the little city they ran to.

All this because of prayer and mercy. What we pray has profound effects. We are the salt in this earth not only in action but in prayer. Know this today – your prayers do make a difference.

God heeds your Word

Daniel 10:12 'Then he said to me, "Do not fear, Daniel, for from the first day that you set your heart to understand, and to humble yourself before your God, your words were heard, and I have come because of your words" '.

What an amazing incident, that God would send an angel to earth **because** of Daniel's **words**. It could be said of Daniel as it was said of Jacob that he had power with God and man.

Daniel however was not the only man to whom God showed such respect. Joshua was battling with the Amorites and needed more daylight to defeat them, so he **spoke to the Lord** and then said, 'Sun, stand still over Ajalon; And moon in the Valley of Ajalon.' And in v.14 it says, 'And there has been no day like that before it or after it, that the Lord **heeded** the **voice** of a **man**; for the Lord fought for Israel.'

God listens and **heeds** the words of man when spoken in faith. 'For assuredly, I say to you, whoever **says** to this mountain, "Be removed and be cast into the sea," and does not doubt in his heart, but believes that those things he **says** will come to pass, he will have whatever he **says**.'

Our words are keys that unlock doors for God to go through and work. As in Daniel's and Joshua's situations, words brought heaven to earth.

When the two blind men came to Jesus he asked them, 'What do you want Me to do for you?' and they **said**, 'Lord, that our eyes may be opened.' They received what they asked for.

In Exodus we read of Moses who asked if he could see God's glory and to this God said, 'I will also **do** this thing that **you have spoken.'**

History has been changed and desires fulfilled all because God heeded men's words. And Jesus is 'the same yesterday, today, and forever.' He is listening to your words. He will **heed** your words. He will move heaven and earth at **your** words as you speak them in accordance with His will and in faith. Be a God-releaser through your words today.

Josh. 10:12, Mk. 11:22, Mt. 20:32–33, Ex. 33:17, Heb. 13:8.

Ordering Your Conversation

Pr. 10:11 'The mouth of the righteous man is a well of life . . .'

What we say can put us **over** or put us under. Proverbs 13:2 says 'A man shall eat by the fruit of his mouth.' Proverbs 15:4 says 'A **wholesome tongue** is a tree of life.' And Proverbs 6:2 says 'You are snared by the **words** of your own **mouth**, you are taken by the **words** of your **mouth**.'

God wants you to succeed, to overcome and to know His saving power. And one primary avenue is by our **words**. Psalm 50:23 KJV says '. . . and to him that **ordereth** his **conversation aright** will I show the salvation of God.' Yes, what we say does make a difference.

Below are several scriptures that will help you overcome. Read them first, then say them out loud. Then memorise them so you can pray them throughout the day. By doing this you will be **ordering** your **conversation aright** and making a way for God's salvation to work in your life.

1 **Cor.** 15:57. 'But thanks be to God, who gives us the victory through our Lord Jesus Christ.'

Phil. 4:13. 'I can do all things through Christ who strengthens me.'

1 **Thess.** 5:24. 'He who calls you is faithful, who also will do it.'

2 **Tim.** 1:8. KJV 'For God has not given us(me) the spirit of fear, but of power and of love and of a sound mind.'

Heb. 13:16. KJV 'The Lord is my helper, and I will not fear what man shall do unto me.'

1 **John** 4:4. KJV 'Ye are of God, little children, and have overcome them, because greater is He that is in you, than he that is in the world.'

Confessing the Answer

Heb. 4:14. 'Seeing then that we have a great High Priest who has passed through the heavens, Jesus the Son of God, let us hold fast to our confession.'

Holding fast to our confession of faith brings the desired results. When Jairus came to Jesus he had a desperate need, his daughter was dying. Yet in spite of his most difficult situation his confession was 'Come and lay your hands on her, that she may be healed, *and she will live.*' His faith **said**, 'and she **will live**.' His words expressed the answer to his need. They were positive words, possibility words, faith words, they were words based on God's ability rather than on man's limitations.

The woman who had the issue of blood for 12 years, who never grew better but only worse, changed her confession when she heard about Jesus. Now her faith said, 'If only I may touch His clothes **I shall be made well**.' From the time she left the house, walked and struggled through the streets, crawled through the crowd and touched Jesus she continually said, 'I shall be made well', and she was!

Begin now to release your faith by speaking the desired result. Confess what God says He'll do in His word and then, 'Hold fast your confession'.

Mt. 9:18, Mt. 9:21, Heb. 4:14.

A Prayer-hearing God

Pr. 15:29 'The Lord is far from the wicked, But He hears the prayer of the righteous'.

Sin separates. It breaks the fellowship, communion and closeness between God and man, and between individuals. David said in Psalm 66:18 'If I regard iniquity in my heart the Lord will not hear.' Isaiah said, 'But your iniquities have separated you from your God; and your sins have hidden His face from you, so that He will not hear.' And Jeremiah said, 'You have covered yourself with a cloud, that prayer should not pass through'.

Prayer is that vital lifeline between God and us and when we allow sin into our lives our pathway to deliverance is cut off. But when we walk by faith, obedience and purity we have the assurance that God **hears** us. And if we know He **hears** us then we know He **answers** us.

With our sin forgiven and placed under the blood, neither man, Satan, nor life, can stop our prayers from being answered. Peter said 'His ears are **open** to their prayers.' Solomon wrote, 'But the prayer of the upright is His delight.' David said, 'The Lord has **heard** my supplication; the Lord **will** receive **my** prayer.' Cornelius was told by an angel that his prayers were **heard**.

We **have** a **prayer-hearing God** who will part the Red Sea, stop the sun and moon, make the sun go back, shut the mouths of lions, destroy the walls of Jericho, unlock the prison doors and carry you away in a chariot to see your prayer answered.

Sin is Satan's tool to deprive us of God's miracles, but righteousness is God's gift to you so you know your prayers are received and answered. Your miracle is waiting for you. God's ears are open and attentive. All that is needed is your prayer offered up with a clean heart and clean hands.

Is. 59:2, 1 Peter 3:12, Pr. 15:8, Ps. 6:9.

Your Squanto is Out There

Mt. 6:8 '. . . For your Father knows the things you have need of before you ask Him'.

When the pilgrims left England to come to America we can be sure that many prayers went up for God's provision. They had launched out into the unknown and did not know what would transpire in the forthcoming months.

Yet the mystery of answered prayer had already been set in motion by God before the pilgrims ever left the shore of their country.

Before settlements began to spring up in North Eastern America, traders frequented it. They would hunt for furs and off-times take Indians to sell as slaves in Europe. In one particular raid they captured an Indian named Squanto who was brought to Spain to be sold. The Monks however, who were against this injustice and cruelty, would go to the slave auctions and buy the Indians, for the purpose of helping them return to their native home. They would teach them English, escort them to England and help them find a passage on a ship back to America.

Squanto was one of these Indians who was bought by the Monks, taught English and eventually found his way back to America. He landed in Maine but his tribe lived in Massachussets so he walked a couple of hundred miles to be reunited with them after all those years.

When he finally arrived he found his entire tribe dead. All had died through disease. It was at this time that the pilgrims were looking for a place to settle. They had landed in Cape Cod but the ground was all sand, the food was scarce and the weather severe. In a small boat this battered remnant landed at Plymouth and made their way up a hill. When they crested the hill they discovered a clearing in the forest, no doubt made by the Indians. With apprehension they made their way into the clearing when suddenly an Indian walked out to meet them. Tension filled the air, stories flooded the pilgrims' minds, until Squanto greeted them in their **native** language – English.

Unknown to them, this was God's answer to all their prayers. Squanto became their friend, educator and guide. He taught them how to survive the winters, farm the land and live in a foreign environment.

God had entered history through the traders, the Monks, the British shipping industry and the heart of Squanto to answer the prayers of His people. And He is **doing** the same for you. Already He is preparing somebody to be the answer to your prayers. He is preparing you to be the answer to someone else's prayers.

God can bring an answer out of any situation, just keep on praying and believing. Your Squanto is out there.

Prayer of Faith for Answered Prayer

O God of my life, hear me and answer me speedily.
  Cut off all my enemies,
  And deliver me from all those who are waiting for me to fail.
In Your righteousness and mercy,
  Save me with Your Right Hand.
By the name of Jesus Your Son, lift me up into Your glory – and establish
  Your Kingdom in me.
Show mankind that You are God,
  and that You answer the prayers of Your people.
I will trust in You, for Your mercy endures forever,
I will cling to Your word more than my life.
Fulfil Your promises to me,
  for I will not let go of Your grace and goodness.
I will not turn away, but wait until I see Your glory.
Set me upon that Rock, show me Your signs and wonders.
Let Your greatness be known to all the world.
I will extol You, for You alone are Truth and Justice.
  You will not fail me.
  Therefore I will trust in none other but You.
I have purposed in my heart, I will not turn back.
  There are no other gods beside You.
  All other help from man is vain.
I will come unto Zion, to Your throne,
  and there You will hear my plea and cause.
You will answer and You will save.
  You will do exceedingly abundantly above all that I ask.
Put my enemies to shame,
  and show them that You are faithful to all who believe in You.
Happy is he who trusts in the Living God.
  You will save, You will perform Your word.
  You will put down the proud and lift up the humble.
In You O God, my Lord and King I will trust.
Though the enemies gather in armies,
  and my friends speak against my prayer.
  Your Spirit will strengthen and sustain me.
I will not fear but trust steadfastly in You alone,
  for great is my confidence in You.
I dance for You are my assurance.
  I praise Your goodness for You are my faith and hope.

(cont.)

I will see the enemy fall,
because You, O God, will vindicate all those who trust in You.
Your Spirit will do the work, for my power comes from You.
You will sustain me in the night,
and give me joy in the day.
You will not disappoint me,
but will show to all that I have prayed according to Your word.
The humble will see and be glad,
but the wicked will grieve and return to the darkness.
I will sing Your praises, for You have heard me and answered me.
You have rent the heavens, scattered all my enemies and set my feet
on the Blessed Rock.
Sing all you peoples, for God has done marvellous things.
Put your trust only in Him, the Maker of heaven and earth.
For by His Son we have been redeemed,
and by His Spirit we are made strong in battle.
O praise the Lord all you lands,
for His mercy endures forever.

by D.C.

Mountain Top Prayer

Luke 21:37 'And in the daytime He was teaching in the temple, but at night He went out and stayed on the mountain called Olivet.'

Jesus learned to **stay on the mountain** of prayer. He did not go from victory to defeat, from glory to discouragement, because He learned the secret of **staying on the mountain** of prayer.

Jesus continually would go to 'a mountain by Himself alone'. When Jesus took Peter, John and James up on the mountain to pray, He was transfigured. Just before Jesus chose the 12 disciples He went to a mountain to pray, 'and continued all night in prayer to God'.

Mountain top praying was not exclusive to just when Jesus was praying in the mountains. Jesus prayed in such a way that regardless of where He was, in the wilderness, on busy streets, in storms or in the company of friends, He maintained that **victorious intimacy** with the Father that **kept Him on the mountain top**.

Moses spent 40 days on the mountain in glorious prayer, but when he came down he still retained the mountain top relationship with God, his face was shining from the glory of God.

The Apostles had a mountain top experience in the upper room after 10 days of prayer – Pentecost. Yet when they left the room they **never lost the glory and the victory**.

And neither do we as we learn to **stay on the mountain** in prayer. Let us begin by climbing the mountain, take one step at a time, one prayer at a time, and if we will not give up we'll make it to the top. Then, once we are there and have learned how to get there, we stay there.

As Moses climbed the mountain he first left the masses, the multitudes who did not want to pray. Then a little further up the 70 elders stopped with Joshua and Hur, but Moses went on up by himself and it says in Exodus 24:16 'Now the glory of the Lord rested on Mount Sinai . . .'.

The Lord is saying to you as He has said to all His other praying children, **'Come up hither'**.

John 6:15, Luke 6:12, Rev. 4:1.

Power in Agreement

Mt. 18:19. 'Again I say to you that if two of you agree on earth concerning anything that they ask, it will be done for them by My Father which is in heaven.'

There is power in agreement. There are results in agreement. One can put a thousand to flight but two can put ten thousand to flight. Solomon wrote, 'Two are better than one, because they have a good reward for their labour. For if they fall, one will lift up his companion. But woe to him who is alone when he falls, For he has no one to help him up. Again, if two lie down together, they will keep warm: But how can one keep warm alone? Though one may be overpowered by another, two can withstand him, And a threefold cord is not quickly broken.'

Without agreement there can be no marriage, friendship, church or peace. Agreement will put power into your prayer life, harmony into your relationships and confidence into your business transactions.

When all the priests and singers were making **one** sound in praise and thanksgiving, the house of the Lord was filled with the glory cloud. As Paul and Silas gave praise and prayer **together** a miraculous deliverance came. Pentecost came at a moment when everybody was in **one** accord in **one** place. No wonder David sang, 'Behold, how **good** and **pleasant** it is, For brethren to dwell **together** in **unity**!'

Jesus points out to us that if we will agree with heaven and with one another then whatever we ask, 'It shall be done.' Our homes can be filled with the glory cloud. Miracles will happen in our lives and the fullness of the Holy Spirit can be our portion.

Make it your first aim to be in agreement with God and His word, then with those around you. In this way 'heaven will come down and glory will fill your soul.'

Ecc. 4:9–12, Ps. 133:1.

Early Morning Prayer

Isaiah 50:4. '. . . He awakens me morning by morning, He awakens my ear to hear as the learned'.

You will find as you read biographies of great men and women of God that early morning prayer was an essential part of their Christian life. Martin Luther said that unless he spent the first four hours of the day with the Lord the devil got the victory.

It is recorded of Jesus that he 'arose a great while before day'. The disciples who were taught by precept and example of Jesus on how to pray also were in the habit of early morning prayer. This habit was then passed on to the early church.

I have found this true in my own life. Morning by morning the Holy Spirit awakens me and we begin to share. Proverbs 6:22 (KJV) says 'Where thou goest, it shall lead thee; when thou sleepest, it shall keep thee; and when thou awakest, it (the Holy Spirit) shall talk with thee.' This is a precious time when the world is quiet and your mind is still untangled in the affairs of the day. This is that 'sweet hour of prayer.' David said, 'O God, You are my God, Early will I seek You.'

This is the hidden secret of men and women who have power with God. While the world cannot see, these people are being renewed by the living Christ. It is here they will receive instruction and strength, it is here they will be fortified for the day's events. This private early morning prayer is like a subterranean current, though it cannot be seen on the surface, life is flowing none-the-less just below.

Can you not hear the Saviour calling, 'Arise, arise, come away my beloved.'

Mk. 1:35 KJV, Ps. 63:1, S. of So. 2:13 KJV.

Morning Prayer

Psalm Seventeen

When morning awakes and the sun arises,
the sparrows begin to sing.
As the Son arises in my heart
so does my voice give way to songs of praise,
for His glory is shed abroad in my heart.

How can the sparrows but sing with the splendour of
the rising sun, with the warmth and light they feel and see.

O that man would rise up early and give praise
for the goodness of our King,
For He is our light of day, the warmth in our soul
the confidence of our hearts.

All the world works within the light and glory of the Son
yet few see the Way, the Truth, and the Life.
Though the Son is faithful, and bright, and glorious.
man rushes on to fill his days with vanity.

All that is required is for one to stop and behold,
to look up and to let the Son fill his heart
with song and rest.
How natural for the sparrow to sing when morning comes.
How responsive is the sparrow's voice to the first
rays of light through the darkness.
How my heart leaps with joy as Jesus my Lord
shines the cords of light and love.
My voice, my mouth is but an instrument.

As I rise in the morning, so must I sing of His mercy
and grace
O to be a sparrow whose nature is to sing at morning's
first light.
Can I be any less?

by D.C.

A Prayer

Psalm Thirteen
Lord, show Your loving-kindness
 and I will praise You!
Give unto me Your light
 and be my path.
Impart Your faith,
 for my confidence has withered away . . .
Show me what is important to Your Kingdom,
 that my kingdom may fade.
Move me from my comfortableness,
 and warm christianity
 to, Your will be done.
Open Your door and close mine behind me.

by D.C.

A Prayer

Psalm Twenty Nine
O reverent Holy Father.
O reverent Holy Father.
Your presence is like the flowers of springtime,
 New and fresh, full of life!
 Awakening my soul with delight!

by D.C.

Death is our Victory

1 Cor. 15:55 'O Death, where is your sting? O Hades, where is your victory?'

Death for most is a chilling passageway to the unknown. But for the overcomer, death is the door to victory.

When one begins to see that death is God's way to freedom and liberty then truly death has lost its sting and bondage. The Hebrew writer said, 'that through **death** He (Jesus) might **destroy** him who had the power of death, that is, the devil, and **release** those who through **fear of death** were all their lifetime subject to bondage.'

It is the fear of death that stops, hinders, immobilises and restricts so many Christians from serving or living for Christ. Christians do not witness or obey Christ in some areas because they are afraid it will **kill** certain relationships or **kill** their reputation.

Yet Jesus said just the opposite, 'if any man will **lose** his life, (will **die to self**) he shall **find** it'. Paul said that 'if we **died** with Christ, we believe that we shall also **live** with **him**.'

The secret of true liberty, true life, true victory and true peace is **death**. Through Jesus Christ we have **died** to sin, **died** to self-will, **died** to the world. And if we believe this, experience this by the **Spirit**, and live in this reality, then that means we are **free** to obey Christ in everything **because we have no fear of what the world thinks or does.**

As long as we are afraid of dying, we shall be afraid of obeying Christ. Paul was not afraid of death in any way. He said, 'to live is Christ, and to die is gain.' Since Jesus was willing to die the Bible says that, 'death no longer has dominion over Him'. Once you have died, you are free. Fellow believer, do not be afraid to die in either your soul-life, self-life, flesh-life or in your physical life. For when we have freely **died to self**, Christ then is enthroned upon our will. And when we die physically, we shall simply shed our bodies and live in the fullness of our redemption.

Oh hear the cry of the overcomers! 'And they did not love their lives (their soul-life and physical life) unto the death.'

Heb. 2:14–15, Mt. 16:25, 2 Tim. 2:11, Phil. 1:21, Rom. 6:9, Rev. 12:11.

Jesus did it for Us

Rom. 6:10 'For the death that He died, He died to sin once for all . . .'.

One morning in prayer I saw Jesus, the Overcomer of overcomers do what I could not, crucify my flesh.

I saw Jesus willingly take my flesh that had been stained with sin and begin to walk the Via Dolorosa. He – and I – were condemned by the Father to death upon the cross. And as He walked toward it I saw everybody cowering away. The disciples fled, the women followed and wept from a distance. The whole world shunned Him, for **who** is willing or even capable of crucifying his own flesh?

I, we – were the disciples, the women, the crowd, who ran from such a fate, and yet it must be suffered. Death of flesh is the only way to a true life of holiness and obedience.

The crowds yelled, 'Crucify Him, crucify Him, away with such a man.' And yet in the heart of Jesus was **us**. I saw how **we** were really crying out to God, **save us, crucify us in Christ, for we cannot save ourselves**.

Then Jesus, as mankind's **self**, was shamed, stripped and mocked, then nailed to the cross. Finally Jesus yielded up His spirit and **self** was dead.

Jesus did what we have all attempted to do, whether through religious zeal, self-discipline, moralism, education or self-denial, namely die to our**selves**. But we have failed because **only Jesus was willing to go the way of the Cross**.

Now like Jesus, if we but yield our spirit up to the Father, He will set us free from our flesh, our**selves**. Paul writes, 'And those who are Christ's have crucified the flesh with its passions and desires.'

Do not run from the cross, it's our pathway to salvation. Look at Christ on the cross and **know** that He **has already liberated us from ourselves**. In this way Christ became our **all**, and through Him we now are overcomers with the Overcomer of the flesh, **self** and sin.

Rest in Him, it's a finished work, the cross has now led us to the throne.

Gal. 5:24.

God in the Opposites

Psalm Fourteen

O, Lord, who can fathom Your wisdom?
You lead Your people through the wilderness
to the Promised Land.
You instruct Your people to give,
so they may receive;
You sent Your Son to bear the penalty of death
that You may bring Life.
You put the silver and gold through the fire
that it might be pure.
You ask us to pardon
that we may be pardoned.
Your church is beaten, hated, killed and cast out
yet it marches on in triumph.

In the belly of the whale Your prophet sang.
When Your people beheld a snake upon a pole
they were healed.
You placed both a harlot and the son of an adulterous
relationship into Your family bloodline.
You created mankind knowing he would fall.

You sent Your Son so He would die.
The way to sin is broad,
but the way to Life is narrow.
In Your Kingdom the least becomes the greatest,
the smallest, the largest.
You, God Almighty, speak in a whisper.
You bring man to his end that he might win.

O, Lord, who can fathom Your wisdom?

by D.C.

The Right 'I'

Ex. 3:14 'And God said to Moses, '**I am who I am**. . .'

One of the most perplexing problems among Christians is the I, me, myself conflict. When God met Moses at the burning bush, he also had an 'I' problem. Notice the two I's in the following conversation between the Lord and Moses.

The Lord said: '*I* have well observed the misery of *my* people in Egypt and *I* have heard this cry . . . for *I* know their sorrows. Now *I* have come down . . . Since the cry of the children of Israel has reached *me* and *I* have observed . . . you come now and *I* will send you . . . that you may bring *my* people . . . out of Egypt.' But Moses said to God, 'Who am *I* to go to Pharaoh?' God said, 'But *I* will accompany you, and this will be your evidence that *I* have sent you.' Moses then asked God, 'When *I* come to the Israelites . . . what shall *I* tell them?'

Here we see two I's, God and Moses. God is continually telling Moses that He is the one who will save Israel, **He** is the one who knows their suffering, He is the one taking responsibility for them, but Moses keeps asking, 'Who am I, how can I do this, what am I to do?' Moses was still so full of I, self and his own consciousness that he couldn't see that he wasn't the one who was going to deliver Israel, **God** would. Moses kept looking at himself while God was telling him to look at Him.

As long as Moses looked at himself he could do nothing else but doubt, question, feel inadequate and stagger at such an unprecedented call to ministry. But finally God ends the subject of 'I's' when He says to Moses, '**I am who I am**'. In other words Moses, there's only **one** I, and that's God.

We too need to learn to forget ourselves, our 'I', and understand that once we are born-again there is a new 'I' dwelling within us, and it's Christ. We died and the 'I' of God became the new us. It is no longer a question of, who are we? Or, what can we do? But it's a recognition of **who God is** and **what God can do**. Once Moses understood this, the **new** Moses went on to become one of the greatest prophets of all history. And once we realise it, we shall no longer be bound by what **we** are or were, but be free to walk in God's greatest.

Whatever we were, we are **not** the same now, for we are new creatures in Christ. There are no ex-divorcees, ex-drug or alcohol addicts, no ex-cons or ex-anything in God's Kingdom, there is only **God** in us, making us new creations.

Ex. 3:7–13 L.B., Ex. 3:14 L.B.

A Poem

Psalm 18

No longer I, but only Christ,
He alone is now my life.
Holy Spirit make this ever new
so out of me flows only You.
Christ my Lord, Christ my all,
help me fulfil my only call
that You alone the world would see,
the lost and hidden eternal key.

by D.C.

Jesus became Sin

2 Cor. 5:21 'For He made Him who knew no sin to be sin for us, that we might become the righteousness of God in Him'.

Just as the Word **became** flesh, so did Jesus **become** sin to redeem us spiritually and physically. The New Berkeley translation says '. . . made sin on our behalf'. Black's translation says '. . . in our behalf God identified him with everything in the whole realm of sin . . .' Wood's translation reads, 'Think of it! Christ the sinless was made the personification of sin for us . . .'. The Jerusalem Bible says, 'For our sake God made the sinless one into sin . . .'

Jesus took our sin, took our place and therefore suffered our death and penalty. The body of Jesus Christ was not only a sacrifice for us but He also died spiritually. He was separated from His body which is physical death, but Jesus was also separated from the Father which is why He cried out, 'Oh God, My God, why hast thou forsaken me?' That was spiritual death, separation from His Father.

Jesus paid the **whole** price for our sin – why? So that we could be set free from sin and Satan. Jesus went into the grave **like us**, so we can come out of the grave **like Him**. Romans 4:25 (Richest translation) says 'As our stand-in He paid the death penalty due us by law for our crimes as our agent; He was restored to Life, making us accepted as though we were as deserving as He'. Jesus took **our sin** and by faith in His resurrection He gives us **His righteousness**.

When we begin to understand that Jesus became like us, taking our sin, then we will begin to see that **we** were raised up and born again in the **likeness of Christ**. That **just as Christ was raised from the dead, so were we. We came out of the grave of sin just as Jesus did**.

The RSV, ASV, NASV, ALF, Young, Weymouth, Amplified and many other Bible translations all say that Jesus was made **alive in the spirit** and when Jesus was made alive in spirit He arose in the Life of God the Conqueror, over sin, sickness, death and Satan. Now listen to Ephesians 2:5 (Amp.) 'Even when we were dead (slain) by (our own) shortcomings and trespasses, He **made us alive together** in fellowship and in union **with Christ** – He gave us the **very life** of Christ Himself, the **same new life with which he quickened him** . . .'.

We were made alive just like Jesus with the same life that Jesus was made alive with, which means we **are conquerors** like Christ. Paul writes, 'For if we have been united together in the likeness of His death, certainly we also **shall be in the likeness of His resurrection**'.

and **in Christ**.

– Glory to God forevermore Amen and Amen –

Luke 27:46 KJV, 1 Peter 3:18, Rom 6:8.*

Believing the 'old man' is dead

Rom. 6:11 'Likewise you also, reckon yourselves to be dead indeed to sin, but alive to God in Christ Jesus our Lord'.

You ask the question, 'If I am a new creation and what I was has passed away, then why am I struggling? Why do I feel as if I'm still unchanged, working through the same problems?'

There are two reasons why many do not experience the joy of living the victorious resurrected life. #1. Ignorance. #2. Faith.

Hosea 4:6 says, 'My people are destroyed for lack of knowledge'. Without revelation knowledge and spiritual understanding of the fact that the old you **has been** crucified, buried, and passed away, you will continue to live as you always did. Our minds have to be enlightened as to what happened in our spirit man.

Secondly, the new man, the new you can **only** live by **faith**, by the **Spirit**, by the **word**. The new man does not live, nor is he governed by the world's system, circumstances or feelings. In other words, faith in God's word and guidance of the Holy Spirit **releases** the new us to function.

Let me give you an example. God's word says the old you has passed away and the new you has been born. You are now faced with the decision of **believing** what God said about you which is seemingly contradictory to how you feel and behave. Our daily sins, frustrations and failures indicate to us that the old man is still very much alive.

Yet here is where we must move from natural reasoning to the reasoning of faith. Faith **believes before** it sees and feels. This is why Paul writes in Rom. 6:11 KJV '**reckon** yourselves to **be dead indeed** to sin, but **alive** to God **in Christ Jesus** our Lord'. By **faith** we are to **see ourselves dead** to sin and alive to God. We're to **regard, count, consider, think**, of ourselves as dead to sin.

It is **only** in the **believing** of this new birth fact that the reality of it will be experienced. The resurrected life can only be lived out in proportion to what we **believe** has died in Christ. We must **believe** our temper has died before peace and patience can resurrect. We must **believe** our old sinful self has died before our new righteous self in Christ will be experienced.

Begin **believing** now that everything you were has passed away and a new you, created in the image and likeness of God has been born. **Think it, see it, act** like it and **believe it. It is an accomplished fact in Christ.**

Our Exchange

Poem

You came to the cross arms opened wide,
  calling me, wooing me to your bleeding side.
On the cross made of sin you hung by cruel spikes,
  stirring my soul with love's greatest sights.
With my knees now in mud made by tears from Your eyes,
  my heart was unchained from Lucifer's lies.
Beholding my Saviour I saw love contained,
  and there at Calvary our vows we exchanged.
Your all for my all, Your life for mine, truly grace beyond
  measure, truly grace divine.
For what could I bring but a splinter of the cross
  the cause of Your death, my release from eternal loss.

by D.C.

Let the old man die

Rom. 6:5 'For if we have been united together in the likeness of His death, certainly we also shall be in the likeness of His resurrection'.

How can we fear our death with Christ when we realize that it was in His death He buried our 'old man.' Our nature that was contaminated with sin, burdened with curses and condemned to an eternal damnation, Jesus the conqueror left in the sepulchre. Our death was swallowed up in the death of deaths, Christ's.

Now we too can join in the song Paul sang. 'O Death, where is your sting? O Hades, where is your victory?'.

As Moses and the Israelites saw the waters drown the Egyptian army in the Red Sea until there was not one of them left, so now in Christ we have seen all of Egypt that was in us buried in the watery grave.

We rejoice in Christ's death for it is the answer by which our release from Satan's grasp is secured. Our old nature along with its sins and enmity against God lies buried behind the grave stone, yet we have risen anew to walk away having 'no more conscience of sins'. We are on the victory side of the empty cross. Our 'old man' is on the other side. 'Therefore we **were** buried with Him through baptism into death, **that just as Christ** was raised from the dead by the glory of the Father, even so we also should **walk in newness of life**. We now bear the image of the resurrected Christ because He bore the image of the sinful nature, the 'old man'. He did what the law could not do, He 'condemned sin in the flesh'. Therefore there is now **no** condemnation (to us) who are in Christ Jesus. Justice was done, the shadowy criminal was executed, so that we could go free.

Should we seek to give shelter to this insidious imposter (the old man) who parades himself as the innocent victim, hiding itself behind morality, religion and psychological cliches like 'I'm O.K., you're O.K. True Christianity originates only from Christ's death. For unless a seed falls into the ground and dies there can be no life.

Waste not another moment, walk the Via Dolorosa with Christ by faith, 'For if we died **with** Christ, we **believe** that we shall also **live with him.' Victory**!!!

1 Cor. 15, Ro. 6:4, Heb. 12:2, Rom. 8:3, Rom. 8:1, Rom. 6:8.

Dead to sin

1 Peter 2:24 'Who Himself bore our sins in His own body on the tree, that we, having died to sins, might live for righteousness – by whose stripes you were healed'.

What does it mean to have 'died to sins', or to be 'dead to sin?'.

Through our union with Christ our 'old man' died and a new man was resurrected. The 'old man' was the one who wanted to sin, to be part of the world and be its own ruler. The old man had his roots in Adam, in rebellion, in selfishness. The new man is rooted in Christ, in obedience, in love. We now desire to do God's will because Christ is the source of our life and being. Our new man, our inner man who is the real redeemed 'us' is **alive** to God, but the old man is now dead, He died when Christ died.

Romans 6:10 says 'For the death that He died, He died to sin once for all; but the life that He lives, He lives to God'. What happened to Christ happened to us so that the death we died was unto sin also. Our old man was placed in a casket and given a funeral. People came to look at him, they stared, some cried and others rejoiced. What people thought and said was unnoticed by our former sinful self. No attention was given to the spectators or people. To them we are now strangers, distant, not there. Why? Because the old man is dead.

This is to be our exact attitude and position toward sin also. We have died to sin, therefore we give it no attention. Though we are tempted by what Satan and people say we pass by uninterested. The former self who at one time would have readily been influenced and enjoyed sin's pleasures is now dead and the new self is **alive to God**.

This spiritual reality is activated by our communion with God, in prayer and in the word. What has already taken place, the funeral of the old self and the resurrection of the new self will become understandable, discernible and practical as we practise walking by faith in daily communion with Him.

Victory march in Christ

Col. 2:15 'And having spoiled principalities and powers He made a show of them openly, triumphing over them.'

Through crucifixion, death and resurrection, Christ conquered the world, the flesh and the devil for us. Hebrews 2:14 says that through death he might **destroy, break the grip, render inoperative, powerless** and **defeat** him that had the power of death, that is, the devil.* Satan **had** power over us but **now, once** we are in Christ, he has none unless we give him some.

In Roman times when a captain defeated his enemies in war he would then march the defeated foes down the streets of Rome as a display to all that he had triumphed over his enemies. And this is what Paul was implying, Christ's victory over Satan and his kingdom. Barclay's translation of Colossians 2:15 reads 'and (He) made a public spectacle of them, as if they had been captives in a victor's triumphal procession.'

Can you see it, Christ, the Captain of our salvation marching the defeated foes, Satan and his demons down the corridors of the spirit realm with all the angels, seraphim and cherubim and saints of old cheering with victorious praise in the grand-stands? Way's translation says 'He disarmed **all** powers and authorities, and made them a public show, and dragged them behind him in the victory-march of Christ'.

Yet the most wondrous story has not been mentioned yet, and that is that **we** were **in Christ, with Christ** when He did this. Which means it was as much **our** victory-march as it was His. All the redeemed were in Christ, triumphantly heading the march of the defeated foe, Satan and his entire band of evil spirits. **In Christ**, we stripped and defeated Satan.

And because of this, 'You have this kind of triumph in life because of your relation to God through Christ' (Johns). Every day we can live triumphantly, every day we can tread the conqueror's path. Every day Christ in us can show the world that we are overcomers.

Translations of Heb. 2:14 in order are Jordan, West, Century, River.*

Death and Resurrection

Rev. 3:21. 'To him who overcomes I will grant to sit with Me on My throne, as I also overcame and sat down with My Father on His throne.'

It is one thing to see Jesus hanging on the cross, being placed in the tomb for burial, resurrected from the dead and sitting down at the Father's right hand. But it takes a leap of faith to see ourselves hanging on the cross, being buried, coming back to life and sitting at the Father's right hand **with** Christ our Lord.

This identification can be seen between Jesus Christ and Joseph. Both were betrayed by ones close to them, both were rejected by family. Jesus died and Joseph was thought to be dead. Jesus was raised from the dead and Joseph was raised out of prison. Jesus sat down at the Father's right hand in power and authority. Joseph was exalted to Pharoah's right hand as ruler over all Egypt. Jesus made himself known to His disciples and Joseph disclosed his identity to his brother also. Jesus sent the Holy Spirit and Joseph sent chariots to his father, both were proof of them being alive.

This divine process of death and resurrection is a settled fact for all believers, but it becomes a living reality (even as it was in Joseph's life) when we 'see' it by faith.

No longer do you have to wrestle with sin's power for in Christ you have died to it. You have now been raised free from sin to live in the resurrection power of Christ. Like Joseph you have been raised to a position of power and authority. We **are** Kings and Priests, we are rulers and masters over the world, the flesh and the devil. **We reign with Christ.**

Just as Joseph had to start **acting** like a ruler so must we. No longer could Joseph be a slave or prisoner and function in his position, and neither can we. Like Joseph, begin to think, act and speak like one who is reigning with Christ, because through the precious work of calvary, **you are seated with Christ in kingship**.

Together With Christ

Col. 2:12. 'Buried with Him in baptism, in which you also were raised with Him through faith in the working of God, who raised Him from the dead.'

I travel quite extensively and therefore see many wonderful sights of God's creation, but my greatest joy comes when my wife is **with** me to share in those experiences. This is why we are married, so we can share life **together**.

God's desire towards man is just the same, He wants us to experience all that He is and all that He does. This is why we are told 'we were buried **with Him**,' we died **with** Him, we were raised **with** Him and we are even seated **with** Christ in heavenly places. When Jesus died on the cross it was not for Himself but for us. Romans 4:28 says, 'Who was delivered for **our** offences and was raised again for **our** justification.'

This is the great mystery of the gospel. We have by faith been linked up **with** Christ in his death, resurrection and glorification. We died to sin **with** Christ, we are raised to newness of life **with** Christ, and now we reign **with** Christ in power and authority over all the enemies of God.

Faith has supernaturally transcended time, distance and man's logic to make us one **with** Christ in His substitutionary work. In God's mind we were all in Christ, one **with** Christ when He died, rose and sat down at the Father's right hand. What happened to Christ happened to us, which is why our 'life is hid **with** Christ in God.' Over and over this wondrous mystery is revealed. 'I am crucified **with** Christ.' He 'Made us alive **together with** Christ'. 'Therefore if we died **with** Christ from the basic principles of the world', we are 'joint-heirs **with** Christ'.

What grace, what mercy, what love, that God has allowed us to experience and share **with** Christ! His death to sin, His victory over all evil and His reign in glory. We are overcomers because we **now** share **with** the Overcomer His total victory.

Rom. 6:4, Col. 3:3, Gal. 2:20, Eph. 2:5, Col. 2:20, Rom. 8:20.

Confessing our Freedom

John 8:36 'Therefore if the Son makes you free, you shall be free indeed'.

Below is a list of comparisons of what we *were* before knowing Christ and what we *are* because of our salvation. Confess them boldly. Accept them as God's grace-gift to you. And then begin to **act** upon them as if they're true.

I was dead in sin, but now I'm alive in Christ
I was prone to sickness, now I'm accustomed to health
I was poor, now I'm prosperous
I was once in darkness, now I'm in the Light
I was defeated, now I'm victorious
I was a sinner, now I'm righteous in Christ
I was a child of the devil, now I'm a child of God
I was in bondage but now I'm free
I used to hate but now I love
I lived in fear and doubt now I walk in faith
I used to lack knowledge but now I have the mind of Christ
I walked in the flesh, now I'm in the Spirit
I was a complainer, now I'm a praiser
I was on my way to hell, now I'm on my way to heaven
I lived by the old man, now I'm a new man
I used to worry but now I live in peace
I was lonely but now Christ is my companion
I was a loser, now I'm a winner
I was headed for the undertaker, but now I'm looking for the uppertaker
I was under the curses but now I'm overtaken with blessings

We were on Satan's ship, but when Christ came into our life we declared **mutiny**! We are taking over now. We were in Satan's prison but now in Christ we are **escapees** . . . We were under Satan's oppressive reign but Christ our Joshua has sounded the cry of **revolution**!

When you confess what God has done for you, you are again proclaiming **mutiny** and **revolution** in Satan's kingdom. Give him no peace, announce his defeat and exalt Christ's victory!

Receiving God's All in Christ

2 Cor. 5:18–19 'Now all things are of God, Who has reconciled us to Himself through Jesus Christ, . . . that is, that God was in Christ reconciling the world to Himself . . .'

Paul caught the revelation that everything God the Father has done for man was accomplished in and through and by Christ. Which means the only way we can receive all that the Father has done for us is by **us being in Christ**.

This is why Jesus said, 'I am the way, the truth and the life. No one comes to the Father **except through me**'. And again, 'Blessed be the God and Father of our Lord Jesus Christ, who has blessed us with **every** spiritual blessing in the heavenly places **in Christ**'. All that the Father has for us is **in Christ**, therefore **we must be in Christ to receive it**. By being in Christ, God and man are brought together to form a union of fellowship.

Paul tells us that God **in** Christ *forgives* us (Eph. 4:32) that God *creates* us **in** Christ Jesus for good works (Eph. 2:10) that God *chose* us **in** Christ (Eph. 1:4) that God has made us *accepted* **in** Christ (Eph. 1:6). God has *adopted* us as sons and daughters **through** Jesus Christ (Eph. 1:5). God gave us an *inheritance* **in** Christ (Eph. 1:11). He sent the *Holy Spirit* **through** Christ (Eph. 1:13). God has shown us His *kindness* **in** Christ (Eph. 2:7). We have been *brought near* to the Father **in** Christ (Eph. 2:13). We have been *reconciled* to God **by** Christ (Eph. 2:16). We have *access* to God **through** Christ (Eph. 2:18). We have been *crucified* **with Christ** (Col. 2:20). We *died* **with** Christ (Rom. 6:5). We were *buried* **with** Christ (Rom 6:4). We have been *resurrected in the likeness* **of** Christ and **with** Christ (Rom. 6:5, Eph. 2:5). We were *raised up* together, and made to *sit together* in heavenly places **in** Christ (Eph. 2:6). God has made us new *creatures* **in** Christ (2 Cor. 5:77). God has made us *righteous* **in** Christ (2 Cor. 5:21). We are **more** than *conquerors* **through** Christ (Rom. 8:37). **In** other words All of God is **in** Christ and we who are **in** Christ receive the All of God. Paul writes 'For in **Him** (Christ) dwells **all** the **fullness** of the Godhead bodily; and **you** are complete **in Him**' (Col. 2:9–10).

John 14:6, Eph. 1:3.

We Are New Creatures

2 Cor. 5:17. 'Therefore if anyone is in Christ, he is a new creation; old things have passed away; behold all things have become new.'

Paul tells us that if any man be **in Christ**, then he is a **new creation**. You are not trying to be or will be, could be, might be or should be but you **are now a new creature**.

This is the good news, the old you was crucified with Christ and a **new** you has been resurrected with Christ. This is the miracle of the new birth.

You received **God's** nature, **God's** heredity, **God's** life and **God's** genetic make-up when you were born-again. This is why we are called sons and daughters of God. We now have a new genealogy. 'You are of **God**, little children . . .' We have been fathered by God and therefore have his nature. We are in the blood line of Christ.

We are now created in the image and likeness of **God**. This is why Jesus, The Son of God, became The Son of Man so that we as sons of man may become sons of God. Now we are being conformed into the image of Jesus Christ. We are going from 'Glory to Glory, just as by the Spirit of the Lord.'

We must begin to see ourselves as God sees us, not as what we **were**. We are different **now** because Christ lives in us by the Holy Spirit. We **have** passed from death unto **life**, we **have** been delivered from the powers of darkness and translated into the kingdom of **Jesus Christ**. **We now have** the **greater one** living inside of us.

No longer do you have to face the world alone, you are a **new creation created** in **righteousness** and **holiness**. Like Paul you can say '**Not I, but Christ**'. Like John you can say, 'because as **He is, so are we in this world**.'

We can **now** walk in the **newness of life, in the likeness of His resurrection** because we have been born of **His incorruptible seed**. The old you has passed away; a new you has come. **Believe it, act like it, rejoice in it**.

1 John 4:4, 2 Cor. 3:18, Gal. 2:28 KJV, 1 John 4:17.

You are Qualified

Colossians 1:12 'giving thanks to the Father who has qualified us to be partakers of the inheritance of the saints in the light.'

How often have we disqualified or eliminated ourselves from doing something, receiving something or becoming somebody? How many people living in ghettos have you heard say 'I'll never get out of here,' when in fact all they must do is walk two miles and they are free of the ghetto. How many feel trapped in an unfulfilled marriage or in a sick body? Because of time, circumstance and pain people unconsciously accept their lot in life and thereby feel unfit to receive the blessing of God.

But Paul brings us good news when he says we have been **qualified, made fit** to partake of the **inheritance** of the saints. Now by virtue of the new birth God has recreated and redesigned you in such a way that you are **able** and **qualified** and **fit** and **deserving** to receive **all** of His blessings.

Now we are **joint-heirs** with Jesus Christ, which means we share in the inheritance He received from the Father after His resurrection. We have been 'blessed with **all** spiritual blessings in heavenly places in Christ.' 'According to His divine power, **He hath given** unto **us all** things that pertain unto **life** and Godliness.'

As a **joint-heir** in Christ you are **now** somebody, you **have received** an inheritance, and you, like Caleb, are 'well able to go up and take the land'.

You have been made fit, qualified and able to partake of the inheritance.

Eph. 1:3 KJV, Num. 13:30 KJV.

Confession: Who we are in Christ

Rom. 10:10 '. . . and with the mouth confession is made unto salvation'.

This confession is not a one time declaration of our faith, but a daily proclamation of what Christ **has** done, is doing and **will** do. Daily confession brings daily salvation, because through our confession we are releasing our prayers, faith, expectation and hopes. Below is a confession that grew out of my personal experience with the Lord. Read it several times with faith, letting the words carry you into a stronger position in Christ.

I know I am a new creature in Christ. His blood has cleansed me from all unrighteousness, my sins have been blotted out, remitted and cast into the sea of forgetfulness. My old nature has been crucified with Christ. I have died with Christ, I was buried with Christ, I was resurrected with Christ, I am seated with Christ in heavenly places **now**, reigning with Him in power and authority. Because I have Christ's nature in me now, His righteousness, His ability, His purity, and His love, I am free from sin, and the flesh with its affections, lusts, deeds and works. I have been delivered from Satan and his power. I now have the life of Christ in me and The Holy Spirit is in me making real the reality of Christ. I have a reborn-spirit, a new heart, therefore I do not desire the old things, for the world is crucified to me. The new me is being renewed daily by the blood and Spirit of Christ. For I have put on the new man, which after God is created in righteousness and true holiness. I have been born of incorruptible seed giving me resurrection life. I have passed from death to life, from the kingdom of darkness to the Kingdom of Jesus my Lord. I now walk in the newness of life. Sin has no dominion over me for the law of the Spirit of life in Christ Jesus has made me free from the law of sin and death. I have Christ's indestructible heredity dwelling in me, making me a world overcomer. His divine nature has made me more than a conqueror. I can do all things through Christ.

Scriptures: Who we are in Christ

This month we want to develop our faith in who we are in Christ. These five scriptures are foundational and will serve as an anchor against feelings of unworthiness and low self-esteem. In Christ the old self-esteem was crucified and we received a new Christ-esteem. All that we are now is because of Christ. Be bold in your confession and allow Christ to rise up in you.

2 Cor. 5:17 'Therefore, if anyone is in Christ, he is a new creation, old things have passed away; behold, all things have become new'

Romans 8:1 'There is therefore **now no** condemnation to those who are in Christ Jesus . . .'

2 Cor. 5:21 L.B 'For God took the sinless Christ and poured into him our sins. Then, in exchange, he poured God's **goodness** into us!'

Gal. 2:20 'I have been crucified with Christ, it is no longer I who live, but Christ lives in me; and the life which I now live in the flesh I live by faith in the Son of God, who loved me and gave Himself for me'.

1 Peter 2:9 Jordan 'But you are a special breed, a noble clergy, a different race, a showstock people, so that you might demonstrate the virtues of the One who called you out of darkness into his dazzling light'.

You are **God's** creation, made in **His** image by the liberating power of Christ's redemptive work. Use these verses daily to remind yourself of the **fact** that you are now 'fearfully and wonderfully made'.

Ps. 139:14.

Christ in Me

Psalm Twenty Two

I will offer my psalm unto You in the early morning,
for my soul is trusting in You.
My soul shall make her boast in You.
My soul will rest in Your goodness,
for Your mercy is ever poured out upon me.
Out of my spirit will I bring forth praise.
From my innermost being come words of adoration and worship,
for it is You who have made Your dwelling place in my heart.
I am a temple of Your holiness, therefore I cannot
but give praise unto Your greatness.
You have made known Your mysteries unto me,
which is Christ in me.
My heart is filled and glad with overflowing joy.
Out of my belly come songs of praise; a new
language which I use to sing unto You.

by D.C.

Christ Our all in all

Col. 3:11. '. . . but Christ is our all in all.'

We are overcomers because Jesus Christ has become everything we need in every situation at all times through the new birth. As you read the following page release your faith to see God become **your all in all**.

He is our **Saviour** from sin's power, **hope** for the hopeless, **health** for sickness, **life** for death, **joy** for sorrow, **strength** for weakness, our **deliverer** from oppression, **freedom** from slavery, **sight** for the blind, a **father to the fatherless, a husband** to the widow, **love** instead of hate, **faith** that conquers fear and doubt. Jesus is our **peace** for confusion, **protection** from trouble, **truth** from deception. He is the **garment of praise** for the spirit of heaviness, **beauty** for ashes, **redemption** for the lost. Our **song** for sadness, **prosperity** for poverty. **El Shaddai** for lack, **wisdom and knowledge** for ignorance. **Heaven** for hell. He is **new** for old things, **faithfulness** to the deserted, a **friend** to the friendless, a **comforter** to those who mourn. He is **power** to the faint, **forgiveness** for our guilt, **acceptance** for rejection, **understanding** to the misunderstood. Jesus is the **way** to the lost, **time** for the hurried, **shelter** for the exposed. Our **anchor** from drifting, **creator** for destruction, **fulfilment** where there are voids, **gentleness** for hardness. Our **good** for bad, **calmness** from storms, **mercy** from due consequences, **justice** for injustice, a **covering** for nakedness, **refuge** from battle, **help** to the helpless, **happiness** from depression, **eagles wings** for the weary, **answers** to our questions, **wholeness** for brokenness, **righteousness** for sinfulness, **relief** from distress, **glory** for shame, **blessings** for curses, **grace for everything**!

Truly, **He is God to you in all things**
at all times in everything!!!
Go in His might

Seated and Reigning together in Christ

Eph. 2:6. 'And raised us up together, and made us sit together in the heavenly places in Christ Jesus.'

After Jesus conquered death, hell and the grave through His death and resurrection, the Father exalted Him by seating Him upon the right hand of His throne. Now Jesus is ruling and reigning as the Son of God and the Son of Man.

Now Jesus is 'far above all principalities, and power, and might, and dominion, and every name that is named . . .' And 'he has put all things under his feet . . .' There is no evil, no demon, no sickness, no problem that Jesus has not conquered. There is no situation that Jesus does not have authority over. Paul says that God has 'highly exalted him, and given him a name which is above every name, that at the name of Jesus every knee should bow . . .' All power and authority has been given unto Jesus who is **now** ruling at the right hand of God.

And the good news is, we who are in Christ are ruling and reigning with Him. We have been raised up **together**, and we are seated **together** in Christ with power and authority.

Therefore, death, hell and the grave are under **our** feet. Satan, his demons, sickness, disease and everything that is beneath Christ is now under us because we are the body of Christ, seated with Him, ruling with Him at the right hand of the Father.

See yourself sitting with Him and by faith begin to reign in Christ over your circumstances, your body, your finances, family, neighbourhood, community and nation. See the Kingdom of God being established through you. See His **will** being done as you begin to live according to Ephesians 2:6, seated **together** in **heavenly** places **in Christ**.

Eph. 1:21, Eph. 1:22 KJV, Phil. 2:19–10 KJV.

Emmanuel

Mt. 1:23 'Behold a virgin shall be with child, and bear a Son, and they shall call His name Immanuel', which is translated, 'God with us'.

When Jesus came to earth He united humanity with Deity. When we come to Christ humanity is once again united with Him. We are not Deity, but through our union with Christ we partake of Deity and live by His grace.

Emmanuel was a prophetic name given to Jesus, it means 'God with us' or 'God manifest in the flesh' . . . Through the union of the new birth Jesus is with us and He is manifesting Himself through our flesh by the Holy Spirit.

Regardless of what time it is, where you are or what circumstances you are encountering, **God is with you to manifest Himself**. He is omnipresent, omnipotent, and omniscient. This means that Jesus Christ our Head is always **all** that He is at **all** times in **all** places in our life. Everything He is and has is available to us at **all** times.

His **allness** is our completeness. We are no longer limited to our own resources, or to what is available to us through our environment. But with Emmanuel we have unlimited, unending, unfailing abundance. Jesus is Lord of **all**. He is Lord of the dead and living, of the Sabbath, the harvest and heaven. Paul says Christ is '**all** in **all**', '**all** might', 'creator of **all** things', '**all** things exist by Him', '**All** things are reconciled by Him', '**All** riches' and '**all** treasures'. There is nothing His **allness** does not cover or provide for.

And if we live **in** His **allness, with** His **allness** and by His **allness**, we shall see His glory. Paul said 'we live and move and have our being in Him'.

We are not alone, God's mystery and loving plan has been revealed. God has placed us in Christ. Emmanuel is not just a name given to Jesus, but it is the reality of our salvation.

Whatever you're facing today, face it with Emmanuel, your **allness** with whom you are united.

Acts 17:28.

Jesus Now

Rev. 1:12–17 'Then I turned to see the voice that spoke with me. And having turned I saw seven golden lampstands, and in the midst of the seven lampstands One like the Son of Man, clothed with a garment down to the feet, and girded about the chest with a golden band. His head and His hair were white like wool, as white as snow, and His eyes like a flame of fire. His feet were like fine brass, as if refined in a furnace, and His voice as the sound of many waters; He had in His right hand seven stars, out of His mouth went a sharp two-edged sword, and His countenance was like the sun shining in its strength. And when I saw Him. I fell at His feet as dead. But he laid His right hand on me saying to me, "Do not be afraid; I am the First and the Last".'

This is a description of the Christ we **now** serve, the One who is seated at the right hand of the Father Who has '**all** power given unto Him in heaven and in earth'.

Jesus is no longer on the earth, He is not upon a cross, He cannot be found in the grave. He has 'spoiled principalities and powers', He 'made a show of them, openly triumphing over them in it'. He has defeated **every** demon, **every** principality, **every** power, **every** creature of hell and Satan. Jesus is the exalted, Sovereign, Almighty God.

He has redeemed us from **every** curse of the law, He has overcome the world with all its tribulations.

Jesus holds the keys of hell and death and has conquered all the enemies of the Church. He is no longer in flesh and blood but He is **God enthroned over all**.

Though the apostles had walked and lived with Jesus, they received a new revelation of Him at Pentecost. They were brought into union with Him so that Christ became **their** Christ, His power **their** power, His miracles **their** miracles.

We need to see Jesus as He is **now**, for this is what changed the apostles' lives. And it will change your life from an historical faith to a **now** faith in a **now** Christ.

Mt. 28:18 KJV, Acts 2:24, Col. 2:15 KJV.

Proverbs

1. The best stories are the ones
   that take a lifetime to tell.

2. Victory and defeat
   both came from within.

3. A man of pride
   will see in others his own faults,
   But a humble man
   will first remove the sin from his own life.

4. God heals the past by
   abundantly blessing the future.

5. Rest is healing.

6. Death is an equal opportunity employer.

7. There is one door for both good and evil: the mouth.

8. Mental illness is like a sandbox on a beach;
   love is like an oasis in a desert.

9. Intimacy comes before warfare in prayer.
   Love comes before security.

10. There are no self-made men in the Kingdom of God,
    only God-made men.

11. In Christ there is victory in every trial,
    in the world there is pride with every victory.

12. God is the cloud maker
    the sun riser
    the rain dropper
    the earth's creator
    the flower bloomer
    the star lighter
    the birds' flight.

by D.C.

The Professional Purger

Psalm 19:12 . . . 'Cleanse me from secret faults.'

My wife has become a professional purger. She will go through the house every six months and eliminate **anything** and **everything** that is not needed or used. Over time it has proved beneficial to our lives because it makes for less clutter, cuts down 'clean up' time and maintains a lifestyle of simplicity. However, purging is not always easy.

One day as my wife was on the purging rampage she was working her way through the house until she arrived in our son's room. Our little boy Joshua, who was only 3½ at that time had seen his mother coming like a white tornado. When she entered the room and began to look around, our little Joshua threw himself in front of his toy shelves with his arms spread out across them and cried out, 'Don't purge my toys mommy, don't purge them'. Needless to say, mommy did not do any more purging that day.

How easy it is for our feet to get covered with dust as we walk the roads of daily life, for our hearts to get weighed down with fears, doubts, cares and wrong thinking. So slow, so invisible, so insidious are these cluttering weights that they're barely perceivable. We get accustomed to living with them.

For two weeks I was wrestling with these weights and did not know why I couldn't break through with victory, until one morning the Purger came in, the Holy Spirit, and in a moment of time **he** cleansed me. My spirit was immediately free, faith and expectation were resurrected again and peace settled into my soul.

Faith is the victory, but as my faith was being buried beneath the clutter, victory was slowly seeping away.

Let the Holy Spirit roll away the stone in you also, and faith will arise. Cluttered lives are suppressed lives, purged lives are liberated lives.

Ministry, Lifestyle, Character

1 Cor. 12:11 'But one and the same Spirit works all these things . . .'.

There are three areas in our life where the Holy Spirit desires to be Lord. They are ministry, lifestyle and character.

Jesus said the Holy Spirit was upon Him **because**, in other words, the Holy Spirit came upon Jesus and **gave Him a specific ministry**; to preach the gospel, heal the broken hearted, preach deliverance, give sight to the blind and set the oppressed free.

The Holy Spirit is more than an anointing for ministry, He also is God and desires to be God in the whole of our lives. Throughout the Bible we can see men who have surrendered to the **way** the Holy Spirit wants to **live** through them.

John the Baptist came wearing camel's hair, eating locusts and honey because this is how the Holy Spirit desired to **live** through John. The Holy Spirit determined John's lifestyle. King David's and King Solomon's lifestyle was also a result of the Holy Spirit's choosing. Abraham became a sojourner, living in tents because it was the lifestyle the Spirit led him to.

Thirdly, the Holy Spirit wants to form our character. Instead of **us** reacting to situations it will be **Christ** in us, by the Spirit living His character out through us. What is the Spirit's character? Love, joy, peace, long suffering, kindness, goodness, faithfulness, gentleness and self-control.

As we walk in the Spirit we shall find that the Holy Spirit will begin to determine more and more the course of our ministry, our lifestyle and character. It's the way of faith and surrender, it's the way of peace. It is also the way of maturity.

It's recognizing **who is God**. The Holy Spirit is a Person with a will and He lives within us **to live His will in His way**. Our part is simply to trust Him and surrender.

Building Up Yourselves

Jude 20. 'But you, beloved, building yourselves up on your most holy faith, praying in the Holy Spirit'.

There is never a reason to be discouraged when you have learned to walk in victory. Never again do you have to settle for feeling empty and lifeless because for every temptation there is a way out.

Many do not recognize feeling empty and lifeless as a temptation but it is. You are tempted to give up, give in or just get by with the minimal amount of effort.

This is not God's way; He is the God of **more than enough**, of doing **abundantly above** all that we ask or think, of supplying **all** our needs according to His riches in **glory**. He desires you to walk as **more than a conqueror**, and we can, as we discover the way out of temptation.

One avenue is 'praying in the Holy Spirit,' or speaking in tongues. Paul says 'He that speaks in a tongue *edifies* himself.' Jude says we **build up ourselves**. As we are praying in tongues, the life of the Holy Spirit begins to flood our spirit and soon we are experiencing the Lord's strength, joy, energy and resurrection power. As Jesus said, out of our belly will flow those rivers of living water.

Paul said he spoke in tongues more than us all. Why? Because amid all the pressures, trials and persecution he needed to be built up, encouraged and uplifted.

Paul was **persuaded** that neither death, nor life, nor angels, nor principalities, nor powers, nor things present, nor things to come, nor height nor depth, nor any other creature, shall be able to separate us from the love of God. Why? Because he had learned **how** to release the resurrected Christ within him into his everyday situation by 'praying in the Holy Spirit'.

Choose to rise above your feelings by speaking to yourselves psalms and hymns and **spiritual** songs. Pray and sing in tongues your whole day through and watch yourselves go from 'glory to glory even as by the Spirit'.

1 Cor. 14:4, 2 Cor. 3:18.

It's our Advantage

John 16:7 'Nevertheless I tell you the truth. It is to your advantage that I go away, for if I do not go away, the Helper will not come to you; but if I depart, I will send Him to you'.

Imagine Jesus, who is God Himself saying, 'It is to your **advantage** that I go away'. How could this be? What could the apostles have wanted more than Jesus in the flesh, personally teaching them?

Jesus desired not only to be with the disciples but also **in** them, and the only way this could happen was for the Holy Spirit to come. In this way the Holy Spirit could produce in the apostles the life and ministry of Christ.

This is why Jesus said, 'Most assuredly, I say to you, he who believes in Me, the works that I do he will do also; and greater works than these he will do, **because I go to my Father**.'

Jesus had to leave in the flesh so that the Holy Spirit who anointed Jesus to do signs, wonders and miracles would now be upon us, His new body to do the **same works**. This is exactly what happened to the disciples in the upper room, which is why they went out and did the same work Jesus had done.

David prophesied this day when he said 'Your people shall be volunteers in the day of your power.' We are in the day of His power, the dispensation of the Holy Spirit, and if we are willing then the works that Jesus did we will do also.

This is the **rest** the Hebrew writers tell us about in Heb. 4:4 'And God rested on the seventh day from all His works'. Now we must rest from our own works of the flesh and self effort and allow the Holy Spirit to minister through us even as He did through Jesus. Jesus said, 'It is the Spirit who gives life; the flesh profits nothing.'

The church and world is in great need for the works of Christ to be made visible again. 'Let us therefore be diligent to enter that rest . . .'. For when we do the world will once again know that Jesus truly is the Son of God.

John 14:12, Ps. 110:3, John 6:63, Heb. 4:11.

Former and Latter Rain

Reading: Mt 12: 24–30 'Let both grow together until the harvest, and at the time of harvest I will say to the reapers, "First gather together the tares and bind them in bundles to burn them, but gather the wheat into my barn".'

There is a maturing process of both good and evil, righteousness and sin, wheat and tares. And the closer we approach the culmination of this age the greater the revival we will see of God's power and Satan's wickedness.

God spoke through Joel saying He would restore to the church the years the locust, cankerworm, caterpillar and palmerworm had eaten. In other words, God is restoring to His church everything Satan has stolen from the Body of Christ over the last 6000 years. The prophet cried, 'For He has given you the former rain faithfully, and he **will** cause the rain to come down for you – the former rain, and the **latter rain** in the first month. The threshing floors shall be **full of wheat**, and the vats shall **overflow** with **new wine** and **oil**'.

God is restoring the former rain (the power given in the Old Testament) and the latter rain (the glory given to the New Testament church) to us. Imagine with me this latter day outpouring of God's mercy where we see everything Adam lost, Israel lost and the church has lost, given back to us in a mounting revival force.

James 5:2 tells us, 'Therefore be patient, brethren, until the coming of the Lord. See how the farmer waits for the precious fruit of the earth, waiting patiently for it until it receives the **early and latter rain**'. Yes, God is beginning to pour out both the early and the latter rains **together**. 'As it was in the days of Noah so shall it be at the coming of the Son of Man.' A flood is coming again, only this time not to destroy but to impower the church to gather in the harvest, the early and latter rain. Don't get caught up on the rising tide of evil but start walking in the outpouring that already started at Pentecost.

Deut 2:23–24, Mt. 24:37 KJV.

Easter's Resurrection

Romans 8:11 'But if the Spirit of him that raised up Jesus from the dead dwell in you, He that raised up Christ from the dead shall also quicken your mortal bodies by his Spirit that dwelleth in you.'

Imagine, the Holy Spirit who raised up Jesus from the dead dwells **in you**. **And**, God has promised that He will **make you alive**, even as He did Jesus with the same resurrection life.

Paul prayed that we might understand this resurrection life, that we might **know** (by experience) what is the exceeding greatness of His power towards us who believe. Because it was this resurrection life that raised Jesus from the dead, lifted Him up and seated Him at the Father's right hand, putting Him above **all** principalities, powers, might, dominion and every name that exists or will exist. It has put **all** things under His feet. And His resurrection Life does the same for us.

This is why Jesus said, 'It is to your **advantage** that I go away, that I may send the comforter (the Holy Spirit)'. It's the Holy Spirit who now quickens, makes alive, imparts resurrection life to us bringing the same results as it did in Christ. He came out of the grave a conqueror over sin, death, Satan, sicknesses, poverty, the world and the flesh – and so have **you**.

'For if we have been planted together in the likeness of his death, **we shall be also in the likeness of His resurrection**.' **You are** above sin, death, Satan, sickness, poverty, the world and the flesh.

There is no problem too big, no power too strong, no trial too great because the Holy Spirit is **in you** to **resurrect you** with His **life**. He will solve every problem every time. He will raise you up, break the cords of bondage and put your enemies under your feet. Now, 'as Christ was raised up from the dead by the glory of the Father, **even so we also should walk in newness of life**' by the Holy Spirit.

John 16:7 KJV, Rom. 6:4 KJV.

Seize your Opportunity

Luke 18:36–38 'And hearing a multitude passing by, he asked what it meant. So they told him that Jesus of Nazareth was passing by. And he cried out, saying, "Jesus, Son of David, have mercy on me!".'

Even though Bartimaeus was a blind man, he still knew **when to seize an opportunity**. Though he had sat at the roadside for years as a beggar he never allowed his condition to quench his desire for freedom. His ears were attuned to the possibilities that might yet bring an answer to his malady.

On this day Bartimaeus **heard** something unusual and immediately inquired of the people what was happening. The response was that Jesus of Nazareth was passing by. Immediately the stories he had heard about Jesus flashed through his mind, and he knew **this was an opportunity to seize**. He then **cried out**, 'Jesus, Son of David, have mercy on me'. The crowds rebuked him, warned him and told him to be quiet, yet Bartimaeus refused to let this opportunity slip through his hand, so he **cried out again**, 'Son of David, have mercy on me'.

Jesus stopped and healed Bartimaeus because he **took the opportunity**. If Bartimaeus had not cried out, Jesus would have kept on going, He would have passed by and an opportunity of a life-time would have been missed.

Faith **seizes opportunities**, but fear only looks and wonders. Faith cries will be heard above the crowds and circumstances, but fear will be buried beneath them both. Faith will not let Jesus pass by, but fear will hide from God. Faith will hear those words, 'What do you want Me to do for you?', but fear will remain in silence. Faith will receive its sight but fear will continue in darkness.

Be attentive, seize opportunities and make every moment of your life count. Jesus is continually passing by and saying to us, 'What do you want Me to do for you?' Our part is to **see Him, believe Him** and **receive from Him**. We don't have to sit in the darkness any longer.

Luke 18:41.

Stand up on your Faith

J.B. Phil. Acts 14:8 'Now it happened one day at Lystra that a man was sitting who had no power in his feet. He had in fact been lame from birth and had never been able to walk. He was listening to Paul as he spoke and Paul, looking him straight in the eye and seeing that he had the faith to be made well, said in a loud voice, 'Stand straight up on your feet'.

The Phillips translation says the man 'sprang to his feet and walked'.

This lame man had faith, only he didn't know how to **activate** his faith. And many times we can be like that. We have faith, yet we sit immobilized because we don't know **what to do**. Paul prayed that the eyes of our understanding would be enlightened because he saw multitudes of Christians idly sitting by while this unlimited inheritance was within them all the time. Like this lame man, we need to be awakened to the potential God has given us.

Gideon didn't know he was a mighty man of valor until the Angel of the Lord told him, the disciples were unaware they could feed the five thousand until Jesus said, 'Feed them'. Moses was startled when God answered his excuses by saying, 'What's in your hand?' That rod he had carried around was found to contain divine power.

And **today** is your day to awaken, to stand straight up, to pick up your rod and **go**! Inside your spirit-man is **God**, the Holy Spirit. On your shelf, table or in your hands is the word of God. Jesus has given us the keys to the Kingdom of Heaven. We **have** the potential, it's all within us, all that remains is for us to **respond to His word** like the lame man, and rise up.

Israel was waiting for Gideon and Moses, the multitudes were waiting for the disciples to feed them, and somebody is waiting for you. Isaiah is saying, '**Awake**, awake! put on your strength O Zion; Put on your beautiful garments, O Jerusalem, the holy city! . . . shake yourself from the dust, arise, . . .'

Take God at His word and **do** what He has called you to do, 'Stand straight up on your feet'.

Is. 52:1–2.

Use Your Own Faith

1 Cor 3:5,7 'Who then is Paul, and who is Apollos, but ministers through whom you believed, as the Lord gave to each one? I planted, Apollos watered, but God gave the increase. So then neither he who plants is anything, nor he who waters, but God who gives the increase'.

How easy it is for us to become followers of man, charismatic leaders or individuals that we admire spiritually. It's a part of one's natural disposition to be dependent upon others, to rely on someone else's faith to solve our difficulties.

But God never intended for a select few to oversee the church, His desire from the beginning is for a nation of priests, a body fully functioning, for all to be believers.

Peter was a fisherman who probably spent more time on his boat than on land. He had learned its limitations and capabilities. He also was acquainted with his fishing companions. Through their work they had established relationships and within this working environment a certain degree of security was achieved.

But one day at sea a storm began to shake their sense of security. All Peter had trusted in, the boat, his companions and experience were failing him. It was then that Jesus appeared walking on the water.

Peter was faced with a choice, to leave his source of security and **step out on his own faith**, or remain close to his boat and friends. And this is exactly what Jesus asks of us all, to leave our world of security, those individuals on whose faith we have been living, and **trust in Christ ourselves**.

To grow in Christ we have to let go of the hand we're holding on to and trust in Christ above all others. He is calling us to do our own praying, our own fasting, our own seeking, our own walking. Do not let the fear of failure hold you back for Jesus is **able to save us to the uttermost**. Our failure will not be sinking in the water after we stepped out, but **not stepping out**.

Use Your Faith

1 John 5:4 'For whatsoever is born of God overcometh the world: and this is the victory that overcometh the world, even our faith.

Faith, the God kind of faith that is in us **is** the **victory** that overcomes the world. Which means if we are going to walk as an overcomer then we must **exercise** it, **use** it, get it **working** for us. Don't let your faith lie dormant, don't let it remain buried beneath the oppression and onslaught of the devil. Take the offensive and **move forward**.

Faith that is hemmed in by fear is very much like a student who studies for an exam. Hour after hour of reading, memorising and writing by the student imprints the knowledge upon his mind. Then the day finally comes for the exam and as the student sits down and sees the questions before him, fear freezes his mind. All of a sudden it seems as though he cannot remember. At this the student may think 'O no, I'm not prepared. I haven't studied enough.' Thoughts of doubt, condemnation and depression fill his mind. What has happened? All the knowledge is in him but fear is blocking his ability to put the answer down on paper. The only thing between the knowledge in his mind and an 'A' on the exam is fear.

And many times the only thing between the faith in us and the answer to our situation is fear also.

What are we to do? **Reject** the **fear as a lie** and **believe that God's faith in us will work**. Say to yourself, I am not going to fail this exam! See Jesus Christ stamp an 'A' on your paper. As the student must recognise that the knowledge within him is the key to the 'A' so must we recognise that the **faith in us is the victory**.

You have the victory, it's God's faith that's in you. Now, push past the fear, condemnation and self-deprecating thoughts by confessing God's word and **walk in victory**.

Abraham's Faith

Rom. 4:17 '. . . even God, who gives life to the dead and calls these things which do not exist as though they did'.

All believers are called to walk in the faith of Abraham. Why? Because his faith worked! It produced results! His was the kind of faith that **pleased** God, **released** God, that **allowed** God to bring the miraculous into his life.

What kind of faith did he have? Word-inspired faith. God gave Abraham a promise, His word that he would have a son 'out of his own bowels' and he **believed.**

God gave the Israelites a promise, His word that they would inherit the land of Canaan. But they did not walk in the faith of Abraham. Hebrews 4:2 says that the word preached did not **profit** them because they did not mix it with faith. They did not please God, or **allow** Him to fulfil His word to them. God had given His word but **they** failed to **mix it** with faith.

God has given us His promise of salvation, healing, deliverance, prosperity and guidance but we must **mix it** with faith. Isaiah 48:12 KJV says 'Thus saith the Lord, thy Redeemer, the Holy One of Israel: I am the Lord thy God, which teacheth thee to profit, which leadeth thee by the way that thou shouldest go'. How could Israel have profited? **By faith**! In what way should they have gone? The way of **faith**!

This was how Abraham profited, he 'staggered **not** at the promises of God through unbelief, but was strong in faith, giving glory to God'.

Unlike the Israelites, Abraham did not allow the deserts in his life to cause him to stagger at God's word because he knew God could 'make the dead alive, and speak the word to those who are yet unborn'. What a secret Abraham discovered that **faith in God's word materializes the promise**. This is why **faith mixed** with the word profits, it brings the promise into **existence**.

You can profit today by **mixing** faith with God's word. It will bring into existence revival, restoration and wholeness for others and yourself. Set your miracle in motion today, **believe His word.**

Rom. 4:20, Rom. 4:17 J.B.Phil.

Strengthened in Faith

Rom. 4:20 'He did not waver at the promise of God through unbelief, but was strengthened in faith, giving glory to God'.

Paul says that Abraham was **strengthened in faith**. This means Abraham **had** faith, but it wasn't strong enough to receive the promised Isaac from God. Therefore he had to **grow** in faith.

The same is true of all Christians, we **have** faith, but it must be **strengthened**, it must **daily grow** in order for us to continually receive from God.

The faith Abraham showed in leaving his country to sojourn in the land of promise was not sufficient to receive Isaac. And the faith we used to receive from God yesterday is also not sufficient to receive from God today. God's desire is **growth**, and therefore with every new promise God wants us to claim, it will require a **stronger** faith.

For a Christian it is not a matter of whether we have or have not faith, but rather the question is, are we willing to exercise it? Abraham exercised his faith, and as he did, it was strengthened until the day came that he received God's gift.

How was his faith strengthened? By not wavering at the promise of God. Abraham held fast to God's word year after year, rejecting doubts, the devil's lies and all outward appearances that were contrary to God's promise. And it was through this process of resisting the devil, resisting his flesh and steadfastly believing God's word that his faith was strengthened.

This is how we're to live by faith also, by simply **believing** God's word, God's promises, and rejecting everything else that is contrary to it.

Has God spoken to you, has He quickened His word to you? Then choose to believe, and in the process of believing, your faith will be strengthened.

Persuaded, Promised, Perform

Rom. 4:21 'And being fully persuaded that, what he had promised, he was able also to perform'.

Paul gives us three faith-filled words describing Abraham's secret for success. They are **persuaded**, **promised** and **perform**. These words are keys to why Abraham's faith worked, and why he can serve as an example of faith for us today.

To be persuaded means one is fully convinced, absolutely certain and firmly convinced. And Abraham was fully assured in his heart that God was giving him a son. Abraham **knew** God, and by understanding His character and abilities he no longer doubted God's word.

Paul's trust in God's promises also came from **knowing God**. He wrote to Timothy saying, 'For I **know who** I have believed and am **persuaded** that He is **able** to keep what I have committed to Him until that Day'.

Secondly, Abraham believed God's promises or word. To Abraham God's word was His bond. God's word constituted absolute authority, it was the final say. The covenant God made with Abraham settled all doubt that God would not and could not fail to keep His promise. God had **sworn** and given Abraham an **oath**. His promises to Abraham were unchangeable.

Thirdly, Abraham **knew** God had the **power** and the **ability** to **perform** His promise. Though it meant a miraculous healing, a reversal of the laws of nature and a regeneration of two old bodies, still he knew God could do it. Abraham had come to believe that all things are possible with God.

When our faith is **persuaded** that what God has **promised** He is able to **perform**, then we shall also see our Isaac. Let us not stagger at His promises, grand and exceedingly great as they are, for He is **able to persuade** us of His willingness to **perform** them. Remember, He has promised **so he can perform**. He has promised because He has the power to do it. All He is desiring from us is **faith**, a faith that is so persuaded by God that it will trust Him under any conditions. Martin Luther, overwhelmed by a promise he had been considering, wrote, 'I forgot God when I said, how can this be?'[1]

2 Tim. 1:12.

[1] 'All the Promises of the Bible', Herbert Lockyer, Zondervan Publishing House, Grand Rapids, Mich. 1962 Page 34.

Don't dig up your Seed

Mk 4:26–28 'And He said, "The Kingdom of God is as if a man should scatter seed on the ground, and should sleep by night and rise by day, and the seed should sprout and grow, he himself does not know how. For the earth yields crops by itself: first the blade, then the head, after that the full grain in the head".'

It was the weekend and my wife and I found ourselves short of cash for a family outing we had decided to take at the last minute. So on our way out of town we stopped at our bank to use the day and night automatic teller. I placed my card into the machine, pressed all the appropriate buttons and then waited.

The wait seemed to be longer than usual. I began to run through my mind any possible errors I might have made. Was the magnetic tape on my card scratched? Did I key in the right number? Was the machine functioning properly?

When I thought I could wait no longer I reached for the button to cancel my request and recover my card, and just before doing it the money came through the slot!

The Lord then spoke to me saying, 'This is what many of my people do, they withdraw their faith just before the miracle happens.'

While in England we gave our car away by selling it to a pastor friend of ours at a low price and then giving the money away. We sowed that car because we were wanting another when we came back the next year. Next year came and we still didn't have a car and so our friend offered to give us the car back. But we said no, because to take the car back would be to dig up our seed. And with no seed you get no crop.

Learn to keep the seed in the ground until you get your crop. Just because you can't see it, doesn't mean it isn't growing. Solomon wrote, 'Cast your bread upon the waters, for you will find it after many days.'

Believe in the seed, then water and care for it and trust the God of miracles to bring the harvest.

Ecc. 11:1.

The Joy of Victory

Psalm Eleven

I awoke with anticipation,
  my spirit alive with my Saviour's expectancy.
You are my Joy, my Faith, my Answer, my Desire.
Surely my prayer has been answered,
  for I know You have heard me.
I shall see the desire of my heart.
My enemies will fall back
  and consternation will be their fill.

As for me, I will give You my morning honorarium.
I will sing Your praises
  for we have seen Your victory!
Your mighty angels have broken through
  with flaming sword, the battle won.
The clouds of witnesses are cheering on.
Let all the saints be glad, and rejoice!

Like Father like son, we are one in purpose,
  sharing the battle, sharing the victory.
Through God we shall do valiantly,
  for in our feet You have trodden down our enemies.

Now I know my God shall supply all my need
  according to His riches in Christ Jesus:
For You are my Shepherd and I do not want.
You are my life-jacket in the stormy sea,
  my resurrection in death,
  my ballast in the depths of the ocean,
  my anchor in the mighty waves.

My joy is complete as Your praises I sing.
My heart is filled with Your victorious, eternal ring!

O Lord my God, my King, Jesus my Saviour
  Your Name is above all the heavens,
  and is renowned in all the earth.
Even in the underworld they tremble when
  Your Name is mentioned!!
Hallelujah

by D.C.

From seed to Fruit

Mt 13:21–31 'The Kingdom of heaven is like a mustard seed, which a man took and sowed in his field, which indeed is the least of all the seeds; but when it is grown it is greater than the herbs and becomes a tree, so that the birds of the air come and nest in its branches'.

When God speaks His word to us or gives us a promise, we very often expect immediate results. Time must then become our teacher, showing that there is a **true season** for His promises.

God's word or promises planted in our human spirit are like seeds that need time, water and prayer-nourishment to mature and develop. Mark 4 talks about the word as a seed, as well as the parable of the tares in Matthew 13.

Our part is learning to differentiate between the seed and the plant. To our thinking we're expecting a fully mature realization of the revelation God has given us, when from God's perspective He had just planted a seed. It is true the seed contains the full potential of the promise, but like all seeds there must be a period of growth.

Smith Wigglesworth was once asked how he acquired such faith, and he answered, 'First the blade, then the ear, after that the full corn in the ear.' His faith had grown and bloomed into full maturity because he cultivated and cared for that mustard seed of faith over the years. He was a wise gardener. But if we are inexperienced gardeners and are constantly looking for the blooms before the plant has matured we shall become discouraged.

There is a time when a gardener has a right to expect fruit from the vineyard, but until then we like Adam and Eve must work with the seed the Lord has planted in our Eden, to ensure that harvest time comes.

Has God given you a promise? Then it is precious seed that needs your attention, **patience**, and care. Your season is coming, the seed is maturing and you will be the first one to partake of its fruit.

Mt. 4:28 KJV.

When the Promise Dies

Cor. 15:36 '. . . what you sow is not made alive unless it dies'.

The life of faith has many surprises, not the least of which is that everything must die before it can live. Faith can become so preoccupied with the answers that it can forget the **process of receiving**.

Jesus gave us the supreme example when He showed us that the way of faith is the way of the cross, as well as the way to resurrection.

Isaac was the promised child through whom all the promises of God to Abraham and His people were to come to pass, yet Abraham was required to sacrifice the promised child. He had to lay even the promise on the altar and let it die. Abraham, our father of faith submitted to this. Why? His faith was not in the promised Isaac but in God. Abraham had learned in the **process of faith** that when **all** possible avenues for God's word or promise to come to pass were eliminated, **God was still able**. God's promise to Abraham was **not** dependent upon Isaac but upon **God**. Therefore Abraham could let even His promised son Isaac die (in a figure) on the altar.

God sends our faith to the cross first so all our sins, weights, false idols and hindrances can be removed, and this makes way for the resurrection.

Has God given you a promise? Then do not fear if even the promise seems to die, for God is only bringing you through the **process of faith** (the cross) to the **resurrection of faith** (the victory). Place your faith in Jesus Christ **alone** and not in what you believe will happen, for only in this way will you know that even when the promise dies you will **see** it resurrected. Though the promise lies in the grave, helpless, lifeless and buried – God **will empty the tomb**. Though the promise lay bound on the altar – **there will be a ram**. Faith in God will bring you through death's corridor and seat you on high with the Overcomer.

God never Fails

Psalm Thirty Five
Let all mankind extol the Lord.
Let the Name of Jesus be lifted up to the highest heavens;
For I will bless and sing and lift up holy hands to You.

I will call upon the Lord to help me,
  and I will praise Him for His answer.
For when I pray He will answer.
And when I make known my requests He will answer.

Therefore I will rejoice, for my God always answers.
He cannot fail me, nor will He leave me forsaken.
He is loyal until Eternity; and His faithfulness will never falter.
He is my confidence and strength.
His unending mercy and goodness are my assurance of answered prayers.

Let all His works be praise: make known all His mighty deeds.
Declare them unto the saints, and let dancing break forth.
Hear creation sing as the Son breaks forth.
His Word is mighty and cannot be changed.
See His handiwork, His glory and His wisdom
  as all of creation breaks forth to life and breath.

Whom has He failed that men can accuse Him?
When did He forget that the birds should not sing?
What promise has He broken that the church cannot plead her cause?
    Tell me: Why does the sun rise day after day?
    and from where did the stars get their light?
Who made the birds to fly and the fish to swim?
Who made man upright to search the ends of the earth?
Who can see the edge of the Universe
  and who has found the beginning of knowledge?
Where are the wise, the scoffers and learned?
In the grave they lie, their thoughts to perish.

But I will look unto my Lord, Creator of all,
  the Source of life and Teacher of secrets.

How can I but sing, for I have found Truth,
  the Living Saviour, Christ Jesus my Lord.
How wondrously He speaks by His Spirit and His Word,
unveiling the path of mankind's journey.

(cont.)

Give praise! Give praise! Sing loudly and jump!
Lift up your hands and clap them in joy!
Dance to His songs and dance in the sanctuary.
Let your voice ring clearly that our Lord is near.
Praise! Praise! Use the instruments of praise.
Praise! Praise! Use the instruments of string.
Praise! Praise! Use the instruments of rhythm.
Praise! Praise! Use the instruments of all lands
Let the new song be sung: give voice to the Spirit.
Give forth from your mouths the praises of heaven.

by D.C.

God Leads in the Paths of Faith

Ex. 14:2 'Speak to the children of Israel, that they turn and camp before Pi Hahiroth, between Migdol and the sea, opposite Baal Zephon; you shall camp before it by the sea'.

There are times when we step out in faith believing we have heard from the Lord only to find ourselves in a situation like the Israelites with the Red Sea before them, mountains on either side and the armies of Pharaoh beating out the sound of death behind them.

An impossible situation! Has God really directed us to this end? It is here in these situations that the quality and strength of our faith in Christ will be revealed.

The Israelites responded by saying, 'Because there were no graves in Egypt, have you taken us away to die in the wilderness?' They accepted no responsibility for their situation, they blamed Moses. They chose to criticise and give vent to their frustration rather than looking to God.

But from the heart of Moses we hear a different voice as he says, 'Do not be afraid. Stand still, and see the salvation of the Lord, which He will accomplish for you today.'

Moses understood that God leads us into paths that **require faith, prayer** and **dependence upon Him**. The Israelites could not see how **they** could deliver themselves, which resulted in them seeing themselves perishing. Moses was not looking to himself but to **God** to be his deliverer which resulted in the **miraculous**.

Has God led you to a Red Sea, then look to **Him** and not yourselves. The devil threw all that he had at the Israelites, yet God triumphed over it all.

Noah trusted God for the rain after building an ark on dry land. Jesus trusted the Father for resurrection life after being led to the cross.

Paul wrote, 'Faithful is He who calls you, who also **will do it**'. Be a Noah, Moses, a disciple, be **in** Christ and **trust God to fulfil his part**.

Ex. 14:11, 14:13. 1 Thess. 5:24 KJV.

Don't Fear, Only Believe

Joshua 1:9 'Have I not **commanded** you? Be strong and of good courage; Be **not afraid**, nor be **dismayed**; for the **Lord** your God is with you wherever you go.'

To our natural minds it would seem as though Peter and Jairus had a reason to be afraid.

When Peter was walking towards Jesus on the water it was in the midst of a raging storm. The waves were crashing all about him, the wind howling, the sky black and threatening and the boat he had just left was struggling for survival. Plus, for a fisherman to walk **on** the water was the most unnatural, unreasonable and illogical thing to do. Did he not have a good reason to fear?

And Jairus, his only daughter whom he loved was deathly ill. There was no medical cure, no known remedy, nothing a father could do. And then the final report came, 'Your daughter is dead.' How these words must have echoed down every chamber of his mind until they pierced his very soul, his love turned to agony, his hopes dashed, his faith crushed. Was not fear to be expected?

Both Peter and Jairus **were on their way to a miracle**. Both had heard Jesus say **yes** to their request. Both were walking in faith until the circumstances became overpowering. Wasn't fear normal under such conditions? **No**! For **Jesus** turned to Peter and said '**Why** are you afraid, O you of **little faith**,' and to Jairus He said, '**Be not afraid, only believe**.'

Jesus expected both of them to **believe**, even in those adverse conditions and he is saying the same to you, '**Why** are you afraid, **only believe**.'

Regardless of your situation, **believe God right now**! In God's eyes there is never a reason to fear but every reason to believe because like Peter and Jairus, **Jesus** was with them the whole time. And when they moved from fear to faith, **salvation came their way**.

Like Peter and Jairus, get your eyes back on Jesus and **only believe**, the miracle is **yours**.

Luke 8:49, Mt. 8:26 KJV. Luke 8:50.

Overcoming Fear Scriptures

This month we want to deal with fear, an emotion or spirit that holds untold millions in captivity. From Genesis to Revelation the word of God continually says to us, 'Fear **not**'.

Jesus came to set us free from fear when He said 'Let **not** your heart be troubled; you believe in God, believe also in Me.' Faith in Jesus Christ dispels all fear for He has conquered every problem, promised never to leave us and will answer our prayers.

As you meditate, memorise and confess these promises, see Christ lifting you out of the waters of fear and setting your feet on a rock that is higher than yourself.

2 Tim. 1:7 KJV 'For God hath **not** given us the spirit of fear; but of **power**, and of **love**, and of a **sound mind.**'

1 John 4:18 KJV 'There is no fear in love, but perfect love **casteth** out all fear.'

Isaiah 4:10 KJV 'Fear thou not, for **I am with thee**: be not dismayed; for I am **thy God**: I will strengthen thee; yea, I will help thee; yea, I will uphold thee with the right hand of my righteousness.'

Isaiah 12:2 KJV 'Behold, God is my salvation; I will trust, and **not be afraid**: for the Lord **Jehovah** is my strength and my song; He also is become my salvation'.

Prov. 1:33 KJV 'But whoso harkeneth unto me shall dwell safely, and shall be quiet from the fear of evil.'

Choose to walk in faith today; when you begin to feel any fear, worry, anxiety or apprehension, immediately pray these scriptures. Keep saying them until faith rises in your heart. Fear is from the devil, faith is from God. Therefore speak faith, think faith and act in faith, then fear will soon fade away.

John 14:1.

Angels, Words and Faith

Hebrews 1:14 'Are they not all ministering spirits sent forth to minister for those who will inherit salvation'.

It is true that God is a mysterious God. Yet it is His will to reveal to His people His mysteries.

This is true concerning faith, prayer and angels. He has revealed these things to us by His Word, and as we understand the mechanics of how God and man work together to build Christ's Kingdom through faith, prayer and angels, we shall find greater success.

When God puts His desires and will into our heart, it is then our responsibility to pray in faith for the realisation of those things. We became God's link on earth for the enlargement and establishment of His Kingdom. It is much like a general with his army sending out an individual on a reconnaissance mission. What those individuals **say** or **report** back to the general will determine when or whether they should engage in battle.

As we pray in faith God despatches His angels to begin working on one particular prayer or Kingdom project. The angels are working on our behalf **because of the faith in our heart and the words we say**. If we **change** our words or abandon our faith we are then giving the angels the message to abandon the project. Daniel's prayer for wisdom was answered **because he maintained his faith and confession for 21 days**. When Gabriel came to Daniel he said, 'and I have come **because of your words**.' Had he changed his words Gabriel would not have come.

We must persevere in faith maintaining our confession until God and His angels have had sufficient time to do **all** that is needed to answer our prayers. Our words and faith create that vital link between heaven and earth, and it is through that agreement that God can work.

When the Israelites gave a **bad report**, God **could not** bring them into the promised land. Maintain your faith and positive confession and you **will see the answer**.

Dan. 10:12.

Scriptures: Angels

We are not alone in the building of God's Kingdom. Christ dwells in us by the Holy Spirit, we are surrounded by a great cloud of witnesses and thirdly, He has created angels to work with us. As we pray, praise, persevere and press towards Christ, His angels are working with us to fulfil His will and promises. Memorize these 5 verses and begin to incorporate them into your prayer life. Angels have been commissioned to minister to **you** just as much as they were to Elisha, Daniel, Jesus and Peter.

Heb. 1:14. 'Are they not all ministering spirits sent forth to minister for those who will inherit salvation?'

Ps 91:11–12. 'For He shall give His angels charge over you, to keep you in all your ways. They shall bear you up in their hands, lest you dash your foot against a stone'.

2 Kings 6:16. 'Do not fear, for those who are with you (angels) are more than those who are with them'.

Ps 34:7. 'The angel of the Lord encamps all around those who fear Him, and delivers them'.

Ex. 23:20. 'Behold, I send an Angel before you to keep you in the way and to bring you into the place which I have prepared'.

Let these verses develop confidence in your heart that God has angels working on your prayer projects, protecting you in your daily life, and even aiding and guiding you. David was so conscious of them that he spoke to them saying, 'Bless the Lord, you His angels, who excel in strength, who do His word, heeding the voice of His word'.

Ps. 103:20.

Jesus Will do it

John 5:7 '. . . Sir, I have no man to put me into the pool when the water is stirred up . . .'

Have you ever felt as though you've come to the end of your faith? You've prayed all your prayers, believed all your faith and tried all you've known to do and yet your situation only grew worse.

There was a certain man who had been incapacitated for 38 years. Like multitudes of other sick people he had waited at the pool of Bethesda for the moving of the waters. When anyone stepped into the waters at that time he was healed. However, this man was so severely sick that he could not even get himself into the water.

Day after day, month after month, year after year he saw his hopes slip away until one day Jesus came and said, 'Do you want to be made well?' To this the man answered correctly, 'Sir, I have **no man to put me into the pool** when the water is stirred up'.

This is a story of compassion, for Jesus did what the man could not do. He put him into the water. He spoke the words of faith and the man was healed.

There was a mother of one son who had come to the end of her food supply. The land was in famine and all resources of food were gone. She had lost all hope and found she could no longer believe. She was about to prepare her last meal and then die.

It was then that our Lord did what she could not, he sent her a prophet, Elijah. Like Jesus to the lame man, Elijah spoke words of faith to the widow of Zarephath and her oil and flour were miraculously multiplied for a year and a half.

Jesus will do what we cannot. Do not fear that your faith may be weak, small or buried behind the rubble of life. Jesus will put you in the water, or send you a prophet. Jesus is still the Author and Finisher of our faith and He will put in what we don't have.

John 5:1.

Faith and Action

James 2:17 'Even so faith, if it hath not works, is dead, being alone.'

A lesson vital to walking in overcoming faith is explained to us by James, and that is: Faith and **action** go hand in hand. You cannot have one without the other and receive from God.

When the disciples were crossing the sea of Galilee they suddenly were caught in a storm, they were **doing** every thing they knew to do to stay alive, except **believe**. You may be caught in a storm of sickness or fear, despair or family problems and you have been doing everything you know to save yourself but like the disciples the situation is only getting worse.

The Lord is saying to you even as He said to Peter, 'Get out of the boat, your boat of sickness or despair and walk towards Me in faith.'

This is where Faith and Action must work together. It will take **faith** to leave your boat, your security, your way of coping with the difficulty and it will take **action** to step out on the waters.

If Peter had never **acted** upon the words of Jesus he never would have known he had walking-on-the-water-faith. And unless you **act** upon the word of God, you will never know whether you have getting-well-faith or overcoming-depression-faith.

Don't belittle or criticise your faith, don't doubt or speak negatively regarding your faith. Simply **step out on it**. As long as you stay in the boat you will never receive. It's time to **act** upon the word of Jesus as He is saying, **'come'**, even as He said to Peter.

You have family-happiness faith, habit-breaking faith, prosperity-faith because you have God's faith in you. Now begin to **walk on your faith**.

Faith Overcomes the World

1 John 5:4 'For whatever is born of God overcomes the world. And this is the victory has overcome the world – our faith.'

Read this verse carefully, 'for whatever is born of God **overcomes the world**!' This means we have been **born to overcome, to win, to conquer, to walk in victory**! The Darby translation reads, 'For **all** that has been begotten of God **gets the victory over the world**.'

A Christian is no longer a born loser but now once in Christ he has become a born winner. The Philips translation reads, 'for God's heredity within us will **always conquer** the world outside us.'

Have you accepted Jesus Christ as your Saviour, are you born-again? Then you **are** an **overcomer**. God has put His life, His heredity, His power, His authority, His ability within you so you are **now** an **overcomer by nature**. 1 John 4:4 says, 'Ye are of God, little children, and have **overcome** them' – **why**? 'Because **greater** is **he** that is **in you** than he that is in the world.'

Now the key to releasing Christ, The Overcomer, who abides in us by the Holy Spirit is faith. 'And **this** is the victory that has overcome the world – our **faith**.' Faith takes the things of God and makes them yours. Faith links you up with **The Overcomer** within.

By **faith** Christ's victory becomes your victory, His power becomes your power, His wisdom your wisdom. **Faith** is the **key** that unlocks the door to all of God's grace. The Philips translation reads, 'In fact, this faith of ours is the **only** way which the world has been conquered.'

Release the Overcomer today by believing that Jesus has **made** you an overcomer by **nature**! As you believe it, think it, practise it and confess it, the Holy Spirit will produce it.

God Kind of Faith

Mk. 11:22–24 KJV. 'Have faith in God. For verily I say unto you, that whosoever shall say unto this mountain, be thou removed, and be thou cast into the sea, and shall not doubt in his heart, but shall believe that those things which he saith shall come to pass; he shall have whatsoever he saith. Therefore I say unto you, what things soever ye desire, when ye pray, believe that ye receive them, and ye shall have them.'

These verses are the Magna Carta of faith. They are the key that will thrust you into a life of the supernatural, for that's what faith does.

When Jesus said 'Have faith in God,' he was also saying 'Have the **faith of God**', or have the **God kind of faith**. What is God's kind of faith? It's the kind of faith that calls those things that are not as though they **were**. It was the kind of faith Jesus exercised when he cursed the fig tree. As far as he was concerned the withering of the tree **was** an accomplished fact, though he did not see the actual physical manifestation until the next day.

The God kind of faith says 'I believe I **have** the answer though I cannot see it or touch it'. Listen to verse 24 again, 'When ye pray, **believe** that ye **receive** them, and ye **shall have** them.' Believing you received is **present tense**, **now**, but **having** it is **future** tense.

I remember when God's faith began to take a hold of my heart. We were in need of $1000.00 for the obstetrician. We needed it that day by 4.00 p.m. and it was now 1.00 p.m. After praying for two hours faith sprang into my heart and I knew that I knew that we **had** the money. I left the office and when I stepped in the door of my house, my very excited wife handed me a cheque for $1085.00. Somebody had given it to her while I was in prayer.

When did I believe? When I was in prayer. I could not see it or touch it but I knew we had it.

Add faith to your prayers, the God kind of faith that puts substance to your hopes and dreams, and as you do you will find your prayer life will **never be the same**.

Faith is the Substance and Evidence

Heb. 11:1 'Now faith is the substance of things hoped for, the evidence of things not seen.'

Faith is an attribute of God, it is real, spiritually tangible and perceivable by our spirit. It is not an intellectual acceptance of a set of principles or a psychological understanding of certain concepts. The kind of faith Hebrews 11 talks about is a divinely inspired attribute of God birthed into our hearts by the Holy Spirit and the word of God.

Faith is self-evident, just as when you fall in love, you **know** it is love. This verse tells us that **faith** is the **substance** and the **evidence** of what you are praying for, **not** the **thing you desire**. The **Amp. Bible** reads (Now faith is the assurance (the confirmation, the title-deed) of the things (we) hope for, being the proof of things (we) do not see and the conviction of their reality-faith perceiving as real fact what is not revealed to the senses.) **Faith** is what tells you that you have what you are praying for. **Faith is your assurance**, **evidence**, **title-deed** that God has said **yes** to your request.

If you were building an extension onto your house you might go to the bank and apply for a loan. If the banker approved your loan and said 'We'll give you the money' – you would begin to act as though the money was yours. You would order building materials, start getting plans and dream how you would decorate the house, even though the money might not be in your account for a few days, weeks or longer. That's faith, and when God says yes to your request, His word will inspire faith in your heart. You will then be able to **believe that you have received**, even though it may be a minute, hour, day, week or year before you actually get it. But regardless of how long it actually takes to have the manifestation in your hand, **faith has become your assurance and evidence that it is yours now**.

Faith Comes by The Word

Romans 11:17. 'So then faith comes by hearing, and hearing by the word of God.'

True faith, God's faith, Bible faith must come from the word of God. If our faith is based on anything else it will crumble and not be able to sustain itself under pressure. But, when God speaks, reveals, quickens his word to you, faith **will** spring up and receive the answer.

The Greek word 'hearing' in Romans 10:17 is 'rhema', which means revelation. In other words, faith comes by revelation, which is God revealing his word to you by the Holy Spirit.

In John chapter 4, there is a story of a nobleman whose son was dying. He came to Jesus imploring Him to come and heal his son before he died. However, Jesus did not go with him but simply **said**, 'Go your way, your son lives!'. Now listen to the nobleman's response 'So the man **believed** the **word** that **Jesus spoke** to him, and he went his way'.

The nobleman **believed** the words of Jesus. Why? Because they came as a revelation, as **truth**. The nobleman had said 'My son is dying', but Jesus said, 'Your son lives.' Two different realities, two different perspectives, yet the man was able to **believe** Jesus more than himself because the **words of Jesus, revealed to his heart, created faith**.

His **faith** was now founded upon **God's infallible, eternal word**, and he was able to walk back home in confidence, **knowing** that his son was well.

Faith based on God's word always brings a happy ending. Like this nobleman, put your faith in God's word and keep it there. Faith grows and feeds on the **living word of God**. As the song writer said, 'All other ground is sinking sand.'

John 4:50.

Faith is Acting Upon the Word

Hebrews 11:4,7,9 'By faith Abel offered . . .' 'By faith Noah . . . moved . . .' 'By faith Abraham . . . went out . . .'

Faith is acting upon the word of God. Faith is **doing** what God has revealed to you or has asked you to do. Faith is simply believing God enough to **obey him**.

The entire eleventh chapter of Hebrews talks about people who **acted** upon God's word to them. Abraham left his home, friends and country to sojourn in the land of Canaan because the **word** of the Lord came to him. Noah built an ark on dry land because he received God's **word**. Sarah's body was healed because she **acted** upon God's **word**. Every time somebody received something from God it was because they had **acted** upon **God's word**. This is what Faith is.

God is challenging you today to start acting upon his **word** in a new way. Don't let all those promises lay dormant in the Bible but begin to let God apply them to your life. **Believe** His word, **act** upon His word, **obey** his word even as Peter did in Luke 5.

The disciples had been fishing all night and had caught nothing. That morning Jesus entered into their boat and **said** to Peter, 'Launch out into the deep and let down your nets for a catch'. Peter replied 'Master, we have toiled all night and caught nothing: nevertheless **at your word I will** let down the net'. Peter **acted** upon Jesus' words, even though experience and circumstances said it wouldn't work. Still he **acted in faith on His word**, and because he did, they took in so many fish the boat began to sink. **Faith in God's word always produces results**.

The Master is speaking to you 'Launch out into the deep'. Step out on His word as the Holy Spirit quickens it to you, and like Peter respond by saying 'nevertheless at your word.' This kind of **faith acting on God's word will** make you an **overcomer**.

Luke 5:4–5.

Seek the Lord

Psalm Thirty Two

Seek the Lord only,
  and in all your seeking you will find Him.
Seek Him first, for He is worthy.
His greatness is to be seen,
  and His love to be understood.

He is the way, He will instruct and guide us
  into His paths of mercy and truth.
All of His paths are peace and rest.

In the darkness of sin man stumbles,
  he is afflicted for his own waywardness;
  he cries and the Lord sends His light.
He takes the scales from man's eyes.

He sets a fire in the sky to guide their path.
He sent them leaders to prepare their hearts.
  He sent His Son to make the way.

Seek the Lord with all your heart,
  as treasures greater than gold or lands.
Seek the Lord all the days of your life,
  for His mercy is everlasting,
  and of His wisdom there is no end.

He led His people to the promised land,
  yet they refused and wandered in a desert place.
He brought them to the border to see His goodness and grace,
  but their eyes were blind and their hearts were hard.
They pitted their way against the way of God.
Destruction came and they gained no understanding.

He sent His Son to a people in captivity,
  to show them the way and loosen their bonds.
They sought not the Lord but took pleasure in their pride.
They hung him on a tree to slay Him,
  to mock and scorn the gift of Light.
Darkness fell, the earth was silent.
The Way had died, the heavens bowed down
  and the angels gave no song.
Smoke filled the Throneroom, God's wrath was poured out,
  the nations cried in pain, the Lamb had been slain.

(cont.)

Scattered were the sheep, in the North, South, East and West.
the nations cried in pain, the Lamb had been slain.
Scattered were the sheep, in the North, South, East and West.
O seek the Lord while He may be found,
for the King of Kings lay in the grave.

The heavens trembled as the Father spoke.
Love flowed from the Throne to the depths of hell.
Christ arose, the Light overcame,
the Way was made into the heart of God.
Seek the Lord for His ways are glorious!
Seek the Lord and His ways become your ways.
Seek the Lord as He sought for you
Seek the Lord and in all your seeking
you shall find the Prince of Peace . . .
Jesus Christ the Living Life!

by D.C.

Receiving

Hebrews. 11:6 'But without faith it is impossible to please Him, for he who comes to God must believe that He is, and that He is a rewarder of those who diligently seek Him'.

Receiving from God takes faith, faith that enables us to endure with patience all the obstacles that appear between our initial desire and the actual physical possession of the desire.

Receiving is a small word, but it's a life-long discipline of faith, perseverance and patience. Jesus tells us seven times in Revelation chapter two and three that the **spoils go to the overcomer**.

Receiving is a simple thing, yet in the spiritual realm it requires the almighty energizing, resurrecting power of God. Jesus 'obtained **our** eternal redemption' by 'the **exceeding greatness** of His **power**'.

The writer of the Epistle to the Hebrews encourages us over and over to maintain a steady faith until we receive **all** God has for us. He warns us that laziness, pulling back, fear and taking our eyes off Christ are serious deterrents to inheriting the promises. The Hebrew Christians were experiencing persecution and the thought of turning back or taking a vacation from confessing their faith was appealing.

Receiving is childlike, yet so all important is it to us as Christians that Jesus died, rose and went before us as a forerunner into the throne of God with His blood to become a surety, and a guarantee that 'All the **promises** of God in Him are **yes** and **Amen**'.

Wherever you are, there is more ground to take, more promises to claim, more of God to experience. The Lord is saying to us, 'Launch out into the deep and let down your nets for a catch, for it is your Father's good pleasure to give **you** the kingdom.'

Heb. 9:12, Eph. 1:19, 2 Cor. 1:20, Luke 5:4, 12:32.

We Release Christ

Luke 17:21 'Nor will they say, "See here!" or "See there!" For indeed, the Kingdom of God is within you'.

In Luke chapter eight, there is a story of the disciples being caught in a fierce storm on the sea of Galilee. So ferocious was the storm that their boat was filled with water and they were in danger of drowning.

Being experienced fishermen I am sure they were doing everything possible to stay afloat, but still their efforts were not enough. Then suddenly it dawned upon Peter that Jesus was asleep below deck. Can you imagine the thoughts and feelings of Peter when he realised this. How can Jesus sleep through the storm? Doesn't He care about us? Why isn't He doing something to help us? When Peter went to wake Him he said, 'Master, don't you care that we're perishing?'

Is this not how we feel when we are in the midst of trials. Why isn't God doing something? Doesn't He realize or see the problem I'm in?

Yet we must learn the same lesson that Peter learned. It wasn't the storm that awoke Jesus, it was **Peter**. It wasn't the problem that moved Jesus into action, it was the faith and heart cry of **Peter**. The Kingdom of God is **within us** even as Jesus was **in** the boat but it wasn't until Peter **recognised** this reality that the **Christ within** rose up and brought about the miracle.

One day Jesus was walking **among** Pharisees and lawyers and the scriptures say, 'and the power of the Lord was present to heal them'. But none of **them** were healed even though they were sick, because they didn't realise that **Christ the healer** was in their midst. However several men carried a paralysed man to Jesus, let him down through the roof because of the crowd, and he was healed, all because they realised Jesus was in **their midst**. **'Stir up the gift that is within**' today and learn to walk in the consciousness of His presence. For it is not problems that release His miracle power, it is prayer and faith.

Mk. 4:38 KJV, Luke 5:17, 2 Tim 1:6 KJV.

Faith Scriptures

Joshua 1:8 'This Book of the Law shall not depart from your mouth . . .'

Below is a list of faith-building scriptures for you to meditate upon, confess and learn this month. It was because Joshua kept the word of God fresh in his life that he was able to remain victorious.

Matt. 18:18 KJV. 'Verily I say unto you, whatsoever ye shall bind on earth shall be bound in heaven: and whatsoever ye shall loose on earth shall be loosed in heaven.'

Mark 9:23 KJV. '. . . If **thou** canst **believe**, **all** things are possible to him that **believeth**.'

Mark 11:22–24 KJV. 'Have the faith of God. For verily I say unto you, That whosoever shall say unto this mountain, Be thou removed, and be thou cast into the sea; and shall not doubt in his heart, but shall **believe** that those things which he saith shall come to pass; he **shall have** whatsoever he saith.' 'Therefore I say unto you, What things soever ye desire, when ye pray, **believe** that ye **receive** them, and ye **shall have** them.'

1 John 5:4 KJV. 'For whatsoever is born of God **overcometh** the world: and this is the **victory** that **overcometh** the world, even our **faith**.'

As you speak these verses out, faith will grow in your heart. Then when you **believe** God's word more than the circumstances you will **see** the answers. **Speak** the word, **meditate** upon the word and then expect the miracles to take place.

Proverbs

1. Without Christ we can do nothing,
   with Christ we can do all things.
   When we have nothing,
   then we have everything.

2. God always leads us in triumph;
   Satan always leads us in defeat.

3. Revelation knowledge is good,
   but it is not synonymous with obedience.

4. Faith in God makes us one with him,
   in purpose, thought and will.

5. For a man with an honest heart,
   failure is the furnace of success.
   But for man with a perverse heart,
   failure is the fire of bitterness.

6. Silence in the midst of many words
   is like a cold breeze on a hot day.

7. Familiarity can lead to
   blindness or clarity.

8. God can do it.
   God will do it.
   God does do it!

9. There is a time in life
   when the hills seem higher
   and the years shorter
   Life is faster, yet you're slower.

10. David could only say,
    It is good to be in the house of the Lord.
    But we can say,
    It is good to **be** the house of the Lord.

11. We must die by faith
    before we can live by faith.

12. In Christ what appears as
    negative is really positive,
    In Satan what appears as
    positive is really negative.

(cont.)

13. Faith has one object: God.
Faith has one path: God's.
Faith has one purpose: God's.

by D.C.

Shout the Victory

Joshua 6:16 '. . . Shout, for the Lord has given you the city!'

Today you can **shout** because the Lord has given you the **victory**. You may be facing walls like Jericho's that seem impenetrable. You've walked around them and from every perspective their formidable greatness has told you they cannot be conquered.

This was true for the Israelites also, which is why they trusted in the Lord and not their own military might. It was not by inventions of war or skill in combat but rather it was their **shout of faith in God**.

When Abijah was king over Judah he was at war with Jereboam the king of Israel. Judah was suddenly caught in a trap between two army divisions of Israel and there was no way of escape. What was Judah's response? 2 Chronicles 13:15 tells us, 'The men of Judah gave a **shout** and **as** the men of Judah **shouted**, it happened that God struck Jereboam and all Israel before Abijah and Judah.'

Joshua and Abijah were able to **shout** before they saw the answer because they **believed God had already given them the victory**. And that is exactly why we can **shout** the **shout** of faith. Jesus has gone before us and taken those Jericho cities of life for us. He **has** delivered us from the power of darkness. We **have** passed from death unto life. He **has** borne our sickness and our pains. He **has** redeemed us from the curse of the law. Our old self **was** crucified. We were made alive together with Christ.

When we **know** Christ has **already overcome** every Jericho and Jereboam we will **shout** too. Turn your attention away from the walls and battle and **shout of victory**.

Psalm 47; 1. Oh, clap your hands, all you people!

Shout unto **God** with the voice of **triumph**!

Every Enemy Destroyed

Ps. 106:9–11 'He rebuked the Red Sea also, and it dried up: so He led them through the depths, As through the wildnerness. He saved them from the hand of him who hated them, And redeemed them from the hand of the enemy. And waters covered their enemies: there was not one of them left.'

There are times in life when it appears the enemy of our soul has us trapped, even as the Israelites were at the Red Sea. The Red Sea lay before us, the mountains engulf us on the East and West and coming up behind us we can hear the pounding hoofbeats of Pharaoh's army.

Yet even in these life crises God is still God. Hear the Prophet cry out 'Behold, the Lord's hand is **not** shortened that it cannot save, nor His ear heavy, that it cannot hear.' Even though the enemy may come in like a flood or a roaring lion, the Spirit of the Lord **will lift up a standard against him.**

God will rebuke your Red Sea, drown **all** your enemies, level your mountains, raise the valleys and make the crooked way straight. This is the miracle of salvation. This is the power of God.

When God answers our cry he doesn't bring advice or suggestions, try to patch up our lives or help us muddle through. He **saves us to the uttermost. He destroys all our enemies. He does a complete work!**

The Israelites saw the Red Sea part, the mountains fade in the background and the entire army of Pharaoh drowned in the sea. **Every** enemy, **every** obstacle, **every problem** was slain and a pathway of deliverance was made.

Jesus came that He might destroy the works of the devil. As someone once said, 'That's His game and victory is His name.' He fought for the Israelites, He'll fight for you. He overcame their Red Sea, He'll overcome yours. Jesus is saying to you as Moses said to the Israelites, 'Do not be afraid. Stand still, and see the salvation of the Lord, which He **will** accomplish for you today.'

Is. 59:1, Ex. 14:13.

Jesus Wins Our Battles

Ps 68:1 'Let God arise, let his enemies be scattered.'

Jesus is The Commander-in-Chief, the Lord of Hosts, who wins our battles for us. As David said, 'He enables us to run through a troop and leap over walls. He strengthens us for battle, teaching our hands for war and our fingers to fight.' Moses said the 'Lord is a man of war'. John saw Jesus riding on a white horse with His robe dipped in blood. The armies of heaven were following Him as He came in the wrath of Almighty God to judge the earth.

From Genesis to Revelation Jesus has never lost a battle. He delivered Noah from a world filled with sin. He saved the Jewish nation by overthrowing Pharaoh's army in the Red Sea. He preserved a godly remnant all through the old testament from nations, sin, famine and war. When Jesus Christ came to earth and went to the cross He forever settled the question of victory as He disarmed principalities and powers, making a public spectacle of them, **triumphing over them**.

Christ's resurrection from the dead proved Him the invincible, unconquerable Warrior. Jesus cannot lose a battle for He is immortal. He lives with death beneath His feet. Truly He is Captain of **our salvation**.

You are not alone in the battle, though a thousand fall at your side and ten thousand at your right hand, He is there to declare: 'stand still and see the salvation of God, *for the battle is not yours, but the Lord's*'.

God will always cause you to triumph in Christ. He is the Defender of the Faith, the Rock of your Salvation, the Mighty One, The Most High Ruler over the Kingdom of Men. As He fought for Moses, Joshua, David, Daniel and Paul, He is fighting for you this very day. Jesus is the Overcomer of your battles.

Ex. 15:3, Col. 2:15, Ex. 14:13, 2 Chron. 20:15.

Deliverance and Protection Scriptures

Psalm 17:4 'Concerning the works of men, by the word of Your lips, I have kept myself from the paths of the destroyer.'

God's word in our mouth is a means of our deliverance and protection. This month the scriptures to meditate, confess and memorise are in the area of deliverance and protection. David said, 'The wicked have laid a snare for me yet I erred not from Thy precepts.'

Job 5:19 KJV 'He shall deliver thee in six troubles, yea in seven there shall no evil touch thee.'

Psalm 18:3 KJV 'I will call upon the Lord who is worthy to be praised: so shall I be saved from mine enemies.'

Psalm 27:5 KJV 'For in the time of trouble he shall hide me in his pavilion: in the secret of his tabernacle shall he hide me: he shall set me up upon a rock.'

Psalm 34:7 KJV 'The Angel of the Lord encampeth round about them that fear him, and delivereth them.'

2 Tim. 4:18 KJV 'And the Lord shall deliver me from every evil work, and will preserve me unto his heavenly kingdom.'

Col. 1:13 KJV 'Who hath delivered us from the power of darkness, and hath translated us into the kingdom of his dear Son.'

God has given you His word. Take it up in your mouth and proclaim it. Like the man who built his house upon the rock, you will remain safe in the time of storms because 'he upholdeth **all things** (which includes you) by the **power of His word**.

Ps 119:110 KJV, Heb. 1:3 KJV.

Let all Nature Praise Him

Psalm Thirty Nine

How mighty is the Lord
who always has a remnant to praise His Holy Name.
He made the sun and stars to ever shine.
proclaiming His wondrous light.
There are birds who always sing
and flowers ever in bloom;
Oceans that clap their waves,
and mountains forever standing tall in strength.
Children ever playing
and bees always buzzing.
How mighty and unfathomable is Your wisdom
creating the heavens and the earth.
At all times there is remnant alive, for the earth is round,
making time a foreshadow of eternity.
Your people are forever praising You in song,
dance and instruments.
From the beginning of time – as long as the earth is round –
a continuous stream of worship and praise
has filled Your throne.
How mighty is Your wisdom,
putting eternity in our hearts.
Let me ever praise my part in Your eternal plan of grace.

by D.C.

High Places in Christ

Psalm 18:33 'He makes my feet like the feet of deer, and sets me on my high places'.

We have been made to walk in **high places**. Not in the low places of lack, discouragement and struggle but in the heavenlies with God, where all that we need is ours.

James tells us, 'Every good gift and every perfect gift is from **above**'. Christ Jesus who sits **above** all is now our source. This is why He has 'raised us **up** together, and made us sit together in the **heavenly places** in Christ Jesus'.

Therefore if we as Christians want or desire anything from God, it must come **down from above**. This is why Paul says, 'If you were raised with Christ, seek those things which are **above**, where Christ is, sitting at the right hand of God. Set your mind on things **above**, not on things on the earth.'

Seeking things below will leave us empty and unsatisfied. The people on earth are fighting, plotting, manipulating and grasping to acquire things. For us God has set another path, the path of simply **being where He is**! As we set our mind on things **above**, as we seek those things which are **above**, then we will live with Christ **above**.

We have been blessed with **every** spiritual blessing in **heavenly places**, not in earthly place. The Hebrew writer tells us if we're in need we're to go boldly to the **throne of grace**. David said, when he was in trouble that God would set him **high** upon a rock. Psalm 91:1 says we're to 'dwell in the secret place of the Most High'.

Refuse to allow life to chain you to the lowlands, soar up on those eagle wings of the Spirit and soar to the Rock that is **higher** than you. Let the words of Jesus be your theme today. 'Look **up** and lift **up** your heads, because your redemption draws near.

Luke 1:17, Eph. 2:6, Col. 3:1–2, Luke 21:28.

Angels at Work

Psalm 91:11 'For He shall give His angels charge over you, To keep you in all your ways.'

Have you ever wondered how Jesus walked upon the water? By angels. Have you ever considered how Jesus could walk through the midst of an angry crowd that wanted to kill him and not be harmed? By angels.

Daniel said that it was an angel sent by God that had closed the mouths of the lions. It was an angel that broke the chains on Peter's hands, opened the prison doors and released him to freedom. It was a host of angels that protected Elisha from the Syrians.

Angels are involved in our lives, and when our eyes have been opened to this truth we will be able to say even as Elisha did, 'Fear not, for they that be with us are more than they that be with them.' The Hebrews writer says, 'Are they not all ministering spirits, sent forth to minister **for them** who shall be heirs of salvation.'

Angels have been commissioned by **God** to help the church establish the Kingdom of Christ. Daniel shows us they help in **answering** our prayers. They can give us **direction** as the angel gave to Philip. They can **strengthen** us as they did Jesus in the garden of Gethsemane. They **deliver** us and help us in bringing people to Christ.

From the beginning of creation until our homecoming with Jesus angels and the church are partners. I'm sure all of us can look back and recall times when we were supernaturally protected. No doubt it was that 'innumerable company of angels' we came into contact with when we entered God's kingdom.

We may not understand how we were saved from various situations, any more than the Israelites understood how all the wheels fell off the Egyptians' chariots when chasing them across the Red Sea. But nonetheless we, like them, know it was God.

No wonder we can live as Overcomers when we have God as our Father, Jesus as our Saviour, the Holy Spirit our indweller and the angels as our helpers.

2 Kings 6:16 KJV, Heb. 1:14 KJV, Heb. 12:22.

Proverbs

1. Action follows words,
   unless the person is a hypocrite.

2. A true lady is one who can adapt
   to any situation.

3. Why talk to a person when he is angry
   You will only get your hand bitten.

4. Christ made our defeat His defeat,
   then He made His victory our victory.

5. By submission a person becomes strong;
   by self-reliance you become weak.

6. On the outside many things look alike,
   but it's the condition of the
   inside that determines the real value.

7. There's a time to fight
   and a time to flee
   A time to persist
   and a time to withdraw
   A time to look
   and a time to turn away
   A time to give
   and a time to receive
   A time to feast
   and a time to fast.

8. Christ went into the grave like us,
   we came out of the grave like Him.

9. The work of God is a proclamation
   of the faith of God.

10. It is not enough to just pray:
    our prayers need signs following.

11. Success comes only one way: God's way.

12. In Your Word are the depths of praise!

by D.C.

Mourning into Dancing

Ps. 30:5 'Weeping may endure for a night, but joy comes in the morning.'

God specialises in bringing **good** out of evil. He's the one who delights in giving us 'beauty for ashes, the oil of joy for mourning, the garment of praise for the spirit of heaviness'.

We have passed from death into **life**, we have been translated from the kingdom of darkness **into** the Kingdom of light. As with Balaam He turns curses into blessings. We have gone from separation to union with Christ. (Ps. 30:11).

From the beginning our God brought life to a dark, void planet. And in the end we read of God once again creating a new heaven and a new earth, free from sin, pain and death.

It was God who took a barren woman named Sarah and made a mighty nation from her offspring. It was God who took a Christian hater named Saul and turned him into a man named Paul who was willing to die for his brother in Christ. It was God who raised His Son Jesus, the man of sorrow, shame and grief from the powers of death, hell and the grave, to the throne where He reigns supreme forever and ever.

Nothing is impossible with God for He alone can turn our sorrow into joy, our weakness into strength, our captivity into freedom. Truly He is the **hope** of **glory**, the **bright morning star**. Jesus is the last **Adam** giving us a second chance. He is the **restorer of the breach**, the **light of the world**, the **resurrection** and the **life**.

Hear Jesus saying to you today even as He spoke to Martha, **'I am the resurrection** and the Life. He who believes in Me though he may die, he **shall live**.' No situation is too hard, no power too great for Jesus Christ to bring good out of it. Jesus arose from the dead that He might be **Lord** both of the **dead** and **living**, so now **His goodness can reign supreme over all**, including you.

Is. 61:3, John 11:25.

Never Give Up

Romans 8:31 '. . . If God be for us, who can be against us.'

After many years and numerous trials, through various dangers and persecutions, when it seemed as though all of hell and man were against Paul, he comes to one conviction, 'If God be for us, who can be against us.' Like a battle cry he declared these words in the face of all opposition because at the end of his life he could say, 'I have fought a good fight, I have **finished the race**, I have kept the faith.'

Regardless of governments and dictators, religious institutions and bigotry, devils and demons, life's necessities and pressures, time or distance, weather or geography, red tape and regulations, dangers or sickness, Paul overcame them all because **God was for him**. Paul allowed nothing to stop him from proclaiming the gospel.

When in prison he took to the pen and witnessed to the guards. On the street he held open-air meetings. He preached in churches and barns, houses and arenas. In the courtroom he shared his testimony, and when totally isolated he prayed. He was an unstoppable firebrand, unceasingly aflame with the message of reconciliation.

In Paul's heart was the greatness and eternality of God, which propelled him beyond anything man, Satan, or life could bring against him. And the same God who was in Paul is in **you**. 'We **have** this **treasure** in earthen vessels, that the excellency of the **power** may be of **God** and not of us.' We are complete in Christ, 'He is our **all in all**.'

As God was for Abraham, David, Paul and Peter, He is **for you**. Therefore 'No weapon formed against you can prosper . . .' for David said, 'For by **thee** I have run through a troop; and by **my God** have I leaped over a wall.' Yes! we **can do all** things through **Christ** who **strengthens** us.

Don't slow down, don't give up, don't give in and don't stop. Regardless of what comes your way today, say as Paul did, 'Knowing that He which raised up the Lord Jesus **shall rise up us** also by Jesus.'

2 Tim. 4:7, 2 Cor. 4:7, Is. 54:17, Ps. 18:19 KJV, 2 Cor. 4:14.

Light Overcomes Darkness

Mt. 4:16. 'The people which sat in darkness saw a great light, and to them which sat in the region and shadow of death light is sprung up.'

God wants us to catch the revelation that light is greater than darkness. Too often we have said to ourselves, 'this is a dark place,' and because of this attitude we feel inadequate and ill equipped to do anything for Jesus.

Yet God has a different perspective. When He looked at planet earth and saw that it was without form, void and dark, He didn't say 'This is a dark place'. No, He said, 'Let there be light, and there was light'.

Thousands of years later when the earth was once again covered with sin, we see God sending His Son into the midst of the darkness. 'And the light shines in the darkness, and the darkness did not comprehend it.' Another translation says 'and overtaketh it not.' Darkness **cannot** overcome **light** in either the spiritual or physical realm.

Jesus the **light** of the world overcame all the darkness he encountered when he healed the sick, raised the dead, cast out demons and preached salvation. Jesus **could not be overcome** and he proved it by His resurrection.

Now we are lights in the world, **now we** are the overcomers and the darkness cannot overtake us, as long as we walk in the light as He is in the light. Regardless of how dark, void or empty the place you may be in, remember that the same **light** that shone through Christ is now **in you**, and **light always overcomes the darkness**.

Paul says, 'For God who commanded the light to **shine out of darkness**, hath **shined** in **our hearts**, to give the light of the knowledge of the glory of God in the face of Jesus Christ.' **Jesus is shining out of you, his glory is being revealed through you**, so that people who sit in great darkness **now** can find Jesus once again – **through you**.

Gen. 1:3, John 1:5, 2 Cor. 4:6 KJV.

Pathway to Glory

2 Cor. 3:18 'But we all, with unveiled face, beholding as in a mirror the glory of the Lord, are being transformed into the same image from glory to glory, just as by the Spirit of the Lord'.

Every step we take in Christ is **forward, upward, victorious** and **glorious**. Growing in Christ is **only** positive. Being changed into God's likeness is always for our good.

Yet sometimes in the process of change we lose sight of the goal and question the validity of God's ways. Moses told the Israelites that God brought them out of Egypt to bring them **in** to the promised land. They wanted deliverance from Egypt, and possession of a land that flowed with milk and honey greatly appealed to them, but the three years in the wilderness was not their idea of going from glory to glory. Their spiritual perception was short-sighted and so they failed to see the wilderness as their *pathway to glory*.

The disciples were eager enough to follow Jesus for they believed Him to be the long awaited Messiah, and the idea of reigning with Him as His close associates when He would overthrow the Roman Empire was to their liking. But when Jesus was crucified on the cross they could not comprehend it to be the very same *avenue to GLORY*.

This is why the Hebrew writer says, 'Now no chastening seems to be joyful for the present, but grievous; nevertheless, afterward it yields the peaceable fruit of righteousness . . .'. Peter writes, 'Beloved, do not think it strange concerning the fiery trial which is to try you, as though some strange thing happened to you; but rejoice to the extent that you partake of Christ's sufferings, that when His **glory** is revealed, you may also be glad with exceeding joy'.

Whether you are in a wilderness, in a trial experiencing His chastisement or all your spiritual aspirations have been shattered, recognize they **are the very corridor to glory, to victory, to growing up into Christ**. For Christ alone turns the negative into positive, the minus into a plus!

Heb. 12:11, 1 Peter 4:12–13.

Walk-on-the-sea-God

Reading John 6:15–21

The disciples' struggle with the storm at sea is similar to the struggles we have with life. Adversities are a reality of living, but they do not have to swallow us up. We have a **walking-on-the-sea God** who when **willingly** received into our hearts as He was into the hearts of the disciples, will **immediately** take us to land.

We have the option of either fighting the storms in our own strength or inviting Jesus into our situation. Jeremiah said 'Oh, Lord God! Behold, You have made the heavens and the earth by Your great power and outstretched arm. There is **nothing too hard for you**' and again 'Behold, I am the Lord, the God of all flesh. Is there anything too hard for Me?'

When Jesus, the Creator of heaven and earth, stepped into the disciples' boat the storm was still raging, the dangers were ever present but the **effects** of it were nullified. They were now **on** the shore. The storm was at a distance. They could stand there and watch it with perfect peace because Jesus had delivered them from its effects.

Jesus did not pray for the Father to take us **out** of the world, rather Jesus came **into** the world to give us victory **over** the world. The only difference between darkness and light, distress and peace, death and life is the **presence of Jesus**. He alone can remove the **effects** of Satan's darts. Invite Jesus into your private conflicts, family problems and daily routine, then watch your **walking-on-the-sea** God bring you to shore, the peaceful shore.

Souls in danger look down, Jesus completely saves,
He will save you by his love out of the angry waves,
He's the Master of the sea billows His will obey,
He your Saviour wants you to be saved today.

Jer. 32:17,27.

Maker of Nature

Psalm Twenty Three

O that men might praise Your goodness and Your
excellency, for You are pure and right.
Your Majesty is glorious to behold and wondrous
to contemplate.

Let all the earth praise Your mighty power, Your
strength and Your righteousness,
for it is You alone, and none other, that have
placed the planets in their orbit.
You have made the stars to shine in the night,
and the sun to make the day.
You have given light to the moon which has no
power to light itself.
Truly the heavens are a display of Your sovereignty.

You cause some birds to fly, and others You have
bound to the earth.
You gave them marshes as a habitation and as a
safe dwelling to raise their young.
With these wings they fly, and with these wings
they cover their young.

How marvellous is Your creation; a wonder to
behold!
Is there any like You in all the earth and heaven?
No! You, alone, are the Almighty, the God of
everlasting Fatherhood, the Saviour of mankind!

by D.C.

Our Ever-present Deliverer

Gal. 1:4 'Who gave himself for our sins, that he might deliver us from this present evil world, according to the will of our God and Father'.

Hear the **will** of our Heavenly Father for us today as He says in this verse: I want you '**delivered from this present evil world**'. Listen again, '**from** this **present** evil world.'

This is not a future deliverance He is talking about, not a promise of escape from some past harrowing experience, but rather an **on-going present tense** deliverance from the ever-pervasive encroaching evil.

By the cross of Jesus Christ we have received deliverance from all **past** evil, and with the promise of His second coming, complete deliverance from future evil will be sure. Yet God's saving promise does not end there, it is **ever present**. His deliverance is yours **now**. David prayed, 'Save **now**, I pray, O Lord; O Lord, I pray, send **now** prosperity'.

When Cain was angry with Abel his brother, the Lord came to him and said, 'Why are you angry? Why is your face downcast? If you do what is right, will you not be accepted? But if you do not do what is right, sin is crouching at your door; it desires to have you, but **you must master it**'.

In this moment of anger God was **present**, and Cain was given wisdom on how to be **delivered** from the present evil crouching at his door. Cain however didn't accept God's ways and so was overcome by sin.

This does not have to be our case, we can learn from Cain's mistake and become **masters** in this **present evil world** by doing what is right, by accepting our Father's ways and allowing Christ's victory over the world to be our victory over the world.

Ps. 118:25, Gen. 4:6–7 NIV.

I am the Resurrection

John 11:25 'Jesus said to her, "I am the resurrection and the life. He who believes in Me, though he may die, he shall live" '.

Martha was faced with the finality of life, the death of her brother Lazarus. For her it was beyond even believing that a miracle could happen. Death had sealed the tomb of all hope and faith. There was nothing left to do but bear the grief.

Then Jesus came, the **I am that I am** and said to Martha, 'Your brother will rise again'. These words were inconceivable to her faith, she could not receive them. They were outside the realm of possibility and light years away from hoping. Jesus however was not daunted by Martha's inability to believe – Jesus is the **same yesterday, today and forever**, He is **the I am** and to Martha in her time of need Jesus was '**I am life**'.

The **power, source** and **creator of life** was standing there before Martha and the **I am that I am is standing before you**. Jesus is the **I am** to give help and meet your need. Even if you're faced with a situation like Martha that is beyond possibility and your faith is shocked beyond belief, Jesus is still the **I am faith** to you. Jesus is the **I am possibility** to you.

Jesus is the ever-present Healer, Giver, Helper, Saviour, Keeper and Joy. There is nothing Jesus is not to lost and hurting mankind.

When Lazarus was raised from the dead, Jesus the **I am** conquered Martha's grief, Lazarus' chains of death, and the unbelief in the multitude who witnessed the resurrection.

Jesus was the Ark to Noah and his family. He was the Mantle to Elisha, the Rod to Moses, the Ram to Abraham. Jesus was the Word to the prophets, the Life to the New Testament Church and He is the one who has **all power in heaven** and **earth** to you.

Jesus the **I am** is with you even as He was with Martha in her most desperate hour of need, and so shall He remain forever and ever.

John 11:23.

Jesus is Lord of Your Dry Bones

Ezekiel 37:5–6 KJV 'Thus saith the Lord God unto these bones; behold, I will cause breath to enter into you, and ye shall live; And I will lay sinews upon you, and will bring up flesh upon you, and cover you with skin, and put breath in you, and ye shall live; and ye shall know that I am the Lord.'

Have you ever felt you were in a dry place, as though your dreams and hopes have fallen apart and there's no more substance to your future? Then take hope in Ezekiel's prophecy which says '**Jesus is Lord of your dry bones**'.

When Ezekiel spoke life into the dry bones he was prophecying the coming of Jesus Christ, who came that we might have **life** and **life more abundantly**. No matter how dry you may be, how dead you may feel, the **life** that raised Jesus from the dry, dead grave is **in you** to resurrect you also.

Secondly, Jesus will put the broken pieces of your dreams back together even as the dry bones linked together again. Though all the king's men cannot put Humpty Dumpty or you back together, Jesus can. If Jesus can take millions of people and form them into a single body called the church, he can rebuild your life, from the inside out.

Thirdly, God put substance on the dry bones flesh. And He has given you substance also. It's called **faith**. 'Faith **is the substance** of things **hoped** for, the **evidence** of things not seen.' God put faith in you at the new birth and even now as you read these words He is inspiring your faith once again. You are being stirred to believe once more.

God has not given up on you. When everybody else, or even you yourself can see nothing but dry bones, the Lord is there to prophesy **life, togetherness** and **substance**.

Jesus Took Our Place

1 Sam. 17:32 'Let no man's heart fail because of him, your servant will go and fight this Philistine.'

The entire army of Israel was immobilised by fear because of a giant warlike soldier named Goliath. Daily Goliath would come to the valley and roar with threats and mockery, challenging and frightening the whole nation of Israel by his appearance and voice. There was not a man in King Saul's great army who was willing to go and fight this Philistine. But God had a man named David, a young man with faith in his heart and God in his soul. When he encountered Goliath, after hearing and seeing his threats, he said to the frightened Israeli army 'Let **no** man's heart fail because of him, your servant will go and fight this Philistine.'

This is exactly what Jesus did for us, He took **our** place and personally defeated, like David, **our Goliaths** by His death, resurrection and glorification. Jesus **spoiled** principalities and powers, He came to **destroy** the works of the devil, He **redeemed** us from the curse of the law, by His **stripes** we were healed, He **delivered** us from fear of death, He has **forgiven** us our sins by His shed blood.

When Saul's army **saw** that David had defeated Goliath, they picked up their arms and rushed towards the Philistines to chase the enemy off their land. And as **you see** with faith that Jesus has defeated your Goliath, **you** can do the same.

Saul's army shared in David's victory, so we share in Christ's victory. No enemy can stand before us, no foe can defeat us, no weapon can prevail against us, for our Goliaths **have been slain**. Our fight of faith is a good fight because we know we win in Christ. Go in this confidence today as a shareholder in Christ's victory over all Goliaths.

Seeking your Goodness

Psalm Twenty Eight

It is You, O Lord, it is You, O Lord, that I have chosen.
I have purposed in my spirit to know and to walk in
Your paths; to search Your Word and
to find Truth.

You have possessed me in my inward parts,
and by Your Spirit You lead my very thoughts and
intentions.
It is You who have turned my path from wickedness
to righteousness.

You are my delight in the morning.
You awaken me to know Your presence.
You teach me secrets and share Your goodness.
O that Your saints would rise up early and seek
Your goodness.

I have inclined my soul to be still that
I might hear Your voice.
I have determind to hold fast Your Word and
to embrace it with my whole heart.
I shall meditate upon Your goodness, for then
shall I give voice to praise.
My faith shall rise to sing of Your faithfulness.

You have taken hold of my life:
Your hands have made known Your plans unto me.
You have revealed Your purposes.

Furthermore, by Your love You have wooed me to
Your side to behold Your grace
How can I but say, Yes, to Your wisdom, O God?
By understanding You have saved me;

By patience You have raised me;
There is none like unto You.
Your ways are marvellous to behold.
O that saints would rise up early and seek Your face.

You are higher than the Heaven of heavens.
Your power, Jehovah, has placed the world in space.
It spins and orbits and keeps time with the galaxies.

(cont.)

You know the depth of the oceans
  and the height of the Universe.
You give directions to those on earth
  who seek you.
My soul rejoices in Your greatness and nearness.

O that Your saints would rise early to praise Your Name:
To acknowledge that You, alone, are Jehovah,
  our Maker and Friend.

by D.C.

Taking Charge

Acts 27:10 'Men I perceive that this voyage will end with disaster and much loss, not only of the cargo and ship, but also our lives.'

There are times in everyone's life when things happen beyond their control. We are still feeling the effects of Adam's sin in the garden. If war is declared in a foreign country we are affected by it. We live in a world that is suffering from the fallout of sin.

Yet, within this 'world of iniquity' that we have found ourselves living in there is still great occasion for rejoicing. God has not allowed the world to go beyond His control and influence. As a matter of fact, 'the earth is (still) the Lord's and the **fullness thereof**'.

Paul was heading into a situation that he knew was going to be dangerous. He warned the ones in authority, but they overrode his opinions. He was then forced to go on being their prisoner, which placed him and all the other 275 men in jeopardy of their lives. (Read Acts 27).

However, Paul was not without recourse, he prayed for 14 days, and was then able to tell the companions, '. . . *take heart* for there will be no loss of life amongst you, but only of the ship. For *there stood by* Me this night an angel of God of whom I belong and whom I serve.'

When everyone else was confused, living in fear and not knowing what to do, when those in authority had come to their wits' end, a Christian **took charge**! Paul told **what** was going to happen and **how** they were going to be saved. In the midst of a world out of control, God was able to **take charge through Paul**.

All through history God has been able to **save, deliver** and **redeem** mankind through people like Noah, Abraham, David and **Jesus**. Now **Christ the Redeemer** is **in you** to help you **take charge**. Don't let the circumstances dictate the outcome, but let **Jesus** the History Maker determine your **salvation**, as well as providing a pathway for others.

Ps. 24:1, Acts 27:22–23.

I Will Day

Psalm 9:1–2 'I will praise You, O Lord, with my whole heart; I will tell of all Your marvellous works. I will be glad and rejoice in You; I will sing praises to Your name, O Most High.'

This is your '**I will**' day. This is your day to choose God's ways over the world's ways, life over death, joy over discouragement. As Joshua said, 'Choose ye this day whom ye will serve,' and you can do so by saying as David did, '**I will** praise You, . . . I will tell . . . I **will** be glad . . . I **will** sing praise to Your name, O Most High.'

Confess the following '**I wills**' of God's word in preparation to the challenges of today.

I will praise you, O Lord. *Ps. 9:1*
I will tell of all your marvellous works.
I will be glad and **rejoice in you**. *Ps 9:2*
I will sing praises to your name, **O most high**.
I will love You, O Lord, my strength. *Ps 18:1*
I will call upon the Lord. *Ps. 18:3*
I will fear no evil. *Ps. 23:4*
I will extol You, O Lord. *Ps. 30:1*
I will bless the Lord at all times. *Ps. 34:1*
I will trust in You. *Ps 56:3*
I will meditate on all Your works. *Ps. 77:12*
I will hear what God the Lord will speak. *Ps. 85:8*
I will walk in Your truth. *Ps. 86:11*
I will worship toward Your holy temple. *Ps. 138:2*

God said 'that if we were **willing** and obedient we would eat the good of the land.' Be **willing** to make God's **will** your will in every aspect of your day.

Josh. 24:15 KJV, Is. 1:19.

Proverbs

1. Put God first and life makes sense.
   Put God last and life has lost its meaning.

2. A liar will keep on lying until his lies devour him.

3. There are no illegitimate
      children in God's family.
   He has Fathered us all.

4. Blaming the Lord is like
      a farmer cursing his land.

5. When a nation is corrupt
      the lawkeeper and poor suffer.

6. A man with secret sins will blackmail
      even his family and closest friends.

7. Right living leads to
      confidence and peace, and hope for tomorrow.

8. A wise man will humble himself and repent.
   He will cry out for help and throw himself upon the Rock.

9. The righteous have songs in their heart,
      but the wicked dance to one continuous dirge.

10. When you walk in the Spirit,
       sin has no power.
    When you walk in the flesh,
       sin's power is revived.

11. Stupidity comes in many shades,
       but the worst is pride.

12. God reserves peace for the humble
       but strife for the egotist.

13. The wicked seek hell
       but the righteous seek heaven.

14. Wealth can be gained by
       giving or taking.

15. Wishing is to laziness
       as believing is to receiving.

by D.C.

Two Boys and a Fence

Psalm 33:20 'Our soul waits for the Lord; He is our help and our shield.'

As I was jogging one day I noticed two young school children leaning over to look through a fence. On the other side of the fence was a dog barking and growling. After a short time the children stood up and continued walking to school. The dog was following them, still barking and growling, jumping up and down and baring his teeth. The children however were undisturbed by all the noise and commotion. Why? Because the dog was on the other side of the fence.

God is our fence, our shield, and like those children, if we stay on His side then we can walk in Christ undisturbed. Paul says to us, '**Above all**, taking the **shield** of **faith** with which you **will** be able to **quench all** the fiery darts of the wicked one.' As long as we hold up our **shield** of faith, the devil can bark and growl, bare his teeth and make a big noise, but we will be safe.

When David was in the midst of battle and his enemies were all around him he sang out to the Lord 'The Lord is my rock and fortress and my deliverer; my God, my strength in whom I will trust; my **shield** and the horn of my salvation, my stronghold.'

When God wanted to calm the fears of Abraham, He said, 'Do not be afraid, Abraham. **I am your shield**, your exceedingly great reward.' In Abraham's situation he needed a shield from the doubts, fears and discouragement that would attack him because he didn't have a child yet.

Whether you need protection from sickness, fear, doubt or family problems, God has promised to be the **shield** for you. Though the devil growls and shows his teeth, remember that the fence is there.

Eph. 6:16, Ps. 18:22, Gen. 15:1.

Resist the Devil

James 4:7 '. . . Resist the devil and he will flee from you.'

Paul says we are not to be ignorant of Satan's devices. He is the father of lies, the deceiver, the accuser of the brethren, the adversary. He comes as an angel of light or a roaring lion.

Yet in Christ we have been given power and authority over **all** the works of the devil. He and his kingdom are now under our feet. Ephesians 1:22–23 tells us 'And He put **all** things under His feet (that's us) and gave Him to be head over **all** things to the church, which is His body, the fullness of Him who fills all in all.'

Now the fullness of Christ dwells in us, His body, His feet, and we can resist the devil successfully and victoriously.

One of the ways we resist the devil is by 'casting down imaginations . . . and bring into captivity every **thought** to the obedience of Christ.' The NIV says we are to 'demolish arguments'. The NAS says we are to destroy 'speculations' and the AMP says 'we refute theories and reasoning'.

Not every thought we think is from us. There are times when the devil whispers his lies, accusations and half-truths to us. Satan beguiled Eve by talking to her. An evil spirit filled Saul's mind with lies about David. Satan even tempted Jesus by presenting speculations and reasoning.

Like Jesus we must reject, cast down, demolish, destroy and refute every thought that is from the devil. We must **resist** him with the mighty weapons of God which are the word, the blood of Jesus, prayer, authority and the whole armour of God.

The next time the devil condemns you, accuses you or lies to you, **resist him**. Say 'In the name of Jesus I reject that thought and command you to leave me.'

Say it with determination and faith. Then, fill your mind with the word of God and praise. You will then find the peace that passeth all understanding will fill your heart and mind again.

2 Cor. 10:5 KJV.

Three Ways Satan Steals

Reading. Mark 4:3–20: The parable of the sower sowing his seed.

In this parable Jesus tells us that the seed is the word of God which is sown in our hearts. However, we are warned that there is an enemy out to steal that word.

Jesus reveals three ways which Satan comes to steal God's word from our lives.

1. Satan and his demons: When Jesus was baptised the Father said to Jesus, 'This is My beloved Son . . .' Immediately Satan came into the wilderness and said, 'If you are the Son of God?' Satan came to bring doubts into Jesus' mind as to whether He really was the Son of God. This is what he does to us when we receive a word from God. He brings his doubts, fear and unbelief tempting us to give up the word.

2. Tribulation or persecution: This is when hard times, trials and people seem to indicate that what you received from the Lord was wrong. And so, because of the constant harassment, we turn back.

3. Cares, deceitfulness of riches, and desires for other things: This includes pressures, anxieties and worries. It is when Satan gets people caught up with the pursuit of the good life that they have no time for God.

The reason why Satan wants to steal the seed or word is because faith comes by the word. Without the word we have nothing to base our faith upon and soon become ineffective Christians. This is why James said, 'Resist the devil and he will flee from you.' 'Fight the good fight of faith.' Jesus said, 'Man shall live by every word of God.'

Have you received the word of the Lord in some area of your life? Then hold fast to it. Treat your heart where the seed was sown like a garden. Protect it, water it and feed it. In this way the seed will grow and produce some 30, 60 or 100 fold.

Soloman said 'keep your heart with all diligence. For out of it spring the issues of life.' Determine today that Satan will never steal any word from you but that you'll keep your heart as good soil, so you can be a fruitful Christian.

Mt. 3:17, Mt. 4:3, James 4:7, 1 Tim. 6:12, Pr. 4:23.

Power to Refuse

Rom. 16:25 'Now to him that is of power to establish you according to my gospel . . .' Scofield.

This is the day that the Lord has made, and this day is an opportunity to achieve His goals by His power. Paul prayed in Colossians that we would be 'strengthened with all might, according to His glorious **power**'. Why? To live in patience, longsuffering and **joy**. Again Paul prayed in Ephesians that we would 'be strengthened with **might** through His Spirit in the inner man', Why? So that we could walk in the love of Christ. In the same book of Ephesians, Paul prayed again that we would know 'the working of His mighty **power**'. And why? So we can walk in dominion over all the enemies of Christ.

It is clear that it takes God's power to achieve God's goals, but if we don't know **how** He wants us to live, nor what is His exceeding **power** that is available to us, then we will tend to take whatever life hands out to us.

If Paul hadn't known it was God's will to go to Rome, then he might have stopped praying during the 14 day storm, and he and all the ship's crew could have died. If the church believed there was nothing they could do against the Roman government when Peter was arrested, then they wouldn't have prayed and Peter's ministry and life would have been over. If the Christians at Joppa thought that Dorcas' death was the will of the Lord she never would have been raised from the dead.

We do not have to accept everything life or the devil hands out to us. Many miracles in the Bible happened because people **refused** to accept the sickness, death or tragedy that came knocking at their door.

Sarah did not accept her barrenness, Bartimaeus did not accept his blindness, Hezekiah rejected that it was time to die. Mordecai refused to accept that the extermination of his race was inevitable. And neither do you need to accept anything the devil brings our way.

God has given us **power** to live an overcoming life of joy. Refuse the works of the enemy and seek God's word to know **what** kind of quality of life He desires you to live.

Eph. 3:16, 1:19.

Tearing down Strongholds

Ps. 144:1 'Blessed be the Lord my Rock, Who trains my hand for war, And my fingers for battle'.

We must realize that we are in a battle, that we are not wrestling against people but against principalities and powers, rulers of darkness and a whole array of spiritual hosts of wickedness.

As we tear down these strongholds of demonic power by the weapons of our warfare, we will see our sons grow up as kings, to walk in righteousness, and our daughters as 'pillars, sculptured in palace style' with godliness and grace. The land will yield its increase and the nations will break forth with gladness and singing.

Spiritual warfare is our spirit empowered by the Holy Spirit battling with evil spirits. It's spirit to spirit, hand to hand combat.

The work of Jesus Christ upon the cross was spiritual warfare, for by His death and resurrection Jesus 'disarmed principalities and powers. He made a public spectacle of them, triumphing over them in it'. It was Satan, the god of this world and the author of sin and death that Jesus defeated by His redemptive work, as well as the forgiveness of our sin through the shedding of His blood. Jesus took the 'Keys of Hades and of Death'. Those keys were in the hands of an evil spirit, the Devil. And, once defeating him, Jesus has freed all humanity, man is now free to accept Christ as his Lord.

We too must get to the source of the problems, the devil and his demons.

Begin to exercise your authority in Christ by using the spiritual weapons in spiritual warfare. Know that you have an enemy who has been defeated by the name and blood of Christ Jesus our Captain of Salvation. We have authority, we have the weapons, now all that remains is our willingness to go to war in the power of the Spirit.

Ps. 144:12, Col. 2:15. Rev. 1:18.

Power over the Enemy

Luke 10:19 'Behold, I give you the authority to trample on serpents and scorpions, and over all the power of the enemy, and nothing shall by any means hurt you'.

Wherever we go or wherever we minister we can know that Satan's power is no stronger in any particular place. There may be a greater manifestation of evil in some places but Satan has a limited power supply. He can only do so much.

But God is **unlimited, almighty, everlasting, eternal**, and **ever-abundant** in power! Satan is no stronger in Africa, America or Japan than he is in Russia, Europe or the Islands. Therefore, as God's children **we** are always in a position of **greater power** than the devil because of our union with Christ, the One who has **all power**.

Wherever we are or wherever we minister, we can overcome and find success in establishing God's Kingdom. When Joshua marched into Canaan it was considered to be the most evil and decadent place on earth, yet God's power in the heart of the Israelites won every battle, and God's Kingdom of righteousness reigned. The tower of Babel, Egypt, Babylon and other nations were Satan's strongholds for evil but they too were all defeated by God's power.

There is no sin so sinful that the blood of Christ cannot wash it clean, no darkness so dark that the light of Christ cannot dispel it. There is no hate so hateful that His love cannot conquer it and no death so dead that His life cannot resurrect it. In Christ we **have** authority over **all** the power of the enemy.

We **can** trample on serpents and scorpions, tread down lions and adders, young lions and dragons. We **can** bind up the strong man and **stand victorious over** principalities and powers, and the rulers of darkness. Our position in Christ has placed us **far** above all of Satan's ability.

We do not need to fear, but rather go anywhere with the knowledge that Christ has given us His ability to cast out demons and demolish demonic strongholds, in order to free the captives and bring them to Christ!

Reigning in Christ's Authority

Gen. 1:26 'Then God said, "Let us make man in Our image, according to Our likeness; Let them have dominion over the fish of the sea, over the birds of the air, and over the cattle, over all the earth and over every creeping thing that creeps on the earth".'

From the beginning God created man in **His** image, gave us **His** authority to carry out **His** will. Man's relationship to God enabled him to rule supreme in complete dominion **over everything** on the earth.

However, through deception and subtlety, Satan usurped man's authority and became 'the god of this world', 'the prince of the power of the air'.

Throughout history we can see, as in a panoramic view, the suffering of mankind because of Satan's harsh dominion.

But Christ, The God of **all authority** and **dominion** broke the power of Satan's reign. And all who accept Jesus as their King and Lord are **delivered** from the powers of darkness and **translated** into the Kingdom of Jesus Christ. No longer are we **under** the ruthless tyrant but now in Christ we are **above** him and have **authority over** him even as Adam had in the garden.

In one moment of faith a twofold divine principle goes into effect. We are loosed from Satan's dominion and placed in authority over him. 1 John 3:8 says 'For **this purpose** the Son of God was manifested, that He might **destroy** the **works** of the devil'. And Hebrews 2:14 says 'that through death He might **destroy** him who **had** the power of death . . .' That word destroy means 'to bring to nought, to render **entirely idle, useless**, to **abolish**, to make of **no** effect, make **void**, to **vanish away**. (Strong's concordance).

This is what happened to Satan's power over us when we were born-again. We have been **restored** to even a higher place than Adam for we reign **with Christ** at the **right hand of God**.

2 Cor. 4:4, Eph. 2:2, Col. 1:13.

Use Spiritual Weapons

2 Cor. 10:3–4 'For though we walk in the flesh, we do not war according to the flesh: For the weapons of our warfare are not carnal but mighty in God for the pulling down of strongholds.'

When David was about to enter into battle with Goliath, Saul's armour was given to him, but it did not fit. From the natural point of view it seemed the logical thing to do. Every soldier wore armour, especially when facing such an opponent as Goliath.

But David knew he was not warring after the flesh but in the spirit, even as we must do. We cannot expect to solve spiritual problems, win spiritual battles and build a spiritual kingdom with carnal means. It is not our talent, intelligence, personal fortitude or natural abilities that bring us victory, but rather 'by **my Spirit**, says the Lord of Hosts.'

We overcome by God's weapons, 'by the blood of the Lamb, and by the word of (our) testimony . . .'. **by** prayer and the whole armour of God. David was so bold because he **knew** he was going to overcome **by the name of the Lord**. Why? Because he had already tested it with the lion and bear.

The Galatians started their battle in the Spirit, but had moved to the flesh and were now losing the battle of faith. Paul had to remind them to pick up their spiritual armour again if they were ever to overcome the enemy, even as David vividly showed the Israelite army that battles were won by God and not by man's weapons.

Like David, let us throw off the armour of Saul, that fleshly protection, and move towards our enemy in faith with God's weapons in our hands, the God who teaches our hands to war, and our fingers to fight.

Then all the world will know that God is in our midst when our Goliath has been conquered with just a sling and a stone. Let **God arise in you and the enemy be scattered**.

Zech. 4:6, Rev. 12:11.

The Light will Conquer

John 1:5 L.B. 'His life is the light that shines through the darkness and the darkness can never extinguish it'.

The struggle between good and evil, light and darkness has been raging since the day Satan sinned. Yet the outcome has long been decided, 'darkness can **never extinguish** light'.

In Genesis 1:2 it says, 'The earth was without form and void; and darkness was on the face of the deep . . .'. Satan thought he had eliminated every trace of God on planet earth yet, in the midst of his delusion God said, 'Let there be light', and **there was light**.

When Satan thought he had defeated Jesus, the light on the cross, in His death and descent into hell, suddenly **light came** and He was resurrected, throwing off the forces of darkness, scattering the hordes of night and 'triumphing over them in it'!

Again, Satan believed he had captured man's spirit, blinded his eyes and separated him from the light. Aimlessly man was wandering, sitting in the darkness and groping in the shadows of sin. But God in His great mercy '**commanded light to shine out of darkness**' and has now '**shone in our hearts to give the light** of the knowledge of the glory of God in the face of Jesus Christ'.

And in the end, when planet earth is facing its final drama, the deceiver will set out to deceive the nations in the four corners of the earth. Satan and his deceivers along with his darkened human slaves will surround the camp of the saints as the sand of the seas. But a light in the form of a fire will come down from heaven and devour them **all**.

Then, **the Light** will descend from heaven with the Holy City, the New Jerusalem; and the Kingdom of **light**, 'the Kingdom of **Christ** will forever be established . . .', there shall be **no** night there. They need no lamp or light of the sun, for the Lord God gives them light. And they shall **reign forever** and **ever**.

Is the light of Christ in you? Then you're on the winning team!

Gen. 1:3, Col. 2:15, 2 Cor. 4:6, Rev. 21:10, Rev. 22:5.

Proverbs

1. To know God
   is to believe God.
   To believe God
   is to obey God.
   To obey God
   is to love God.
   To love God
   is to know God.

2. Time has no value,
   It's only what we do
   or don't do within
   the will of God
   that gives time purpose.

3. The present generation
   shows the sins of the
   former generation.

4. Faith is not the ultimate: **God** is!

5. The flesh wears pride on its sleeve,
   But the spirit man carries
   a cross on its heart.

6. A nation will rise to greatness
   when leaders lead righteously
   and the people follow willingly.

7. The external is dependent
   upon the internal.
   The crop is determined
   by what's beneath the soil.
   The visible is contingent
   upon the invisible.
   All things exist, and have
   their being because of God.

8. You are the joy of my heart,
   the life of my spirit,
   the thoughts of my mind
   and the volition of my will.
   You are the motive of my desires,
   the source of my intentions.

(cont.)

You alone are the value of my life
  and the length of my days,
  the sculptor in my hands,
  the direction in my step.
You're the song of my soul
  and the words of my mouth.
The focus of my eyes
  and the sound in my ears.
The treasure in this vessel,
  the fragrance of my scent.

9. I have only one prayer:
  that my oneness with You, Christ,
  would be lived.

by D.C.

Jesus went to Heal

Mt. 4:23 'Now Jesus went about all Galilee, teaching in their synagogues, preaching the gospel of the Kingdom, and healing all kinds of sickness and all kinds of diseases among the people'.

From beginning to end of the four gospels we can see Jesus as the Healer. Never do we find anyone not receiving their healing when they came to Jesus with faith. And why was this? Because Matthew 4:23 tells us Jesus **went** about . . . 'healing all manner of sicknesses and all manner of diseases.'

Jesus **went** to heal, as well as to teach and preach. Matthew 9:35 says that 'Jesus **went** about all the cities and villages . . . healing every sickness and every disease . . .' Matthew 14:14 says 'Jesus **went** forth . . . and he healed their sick'. Matthew 15:29–31 tells us 'Jesus . . . **went** along by lake Galilee' and great multitudes were healed. John 5:1 says that Jesus '**went** up to Jerusalem to the pool of Bethesda' – why? To heal the man whose infirmity had lasted 38 years. Again in Mark 6:56 it says that **whithersoever** Jesus **went** – villages, cities, country, synagogues, mountains or deserts, people were **healed**. Yes, Jesus **went** to heal, not to condemn, destroy, hurt or prolong suffering. And He is the **same today** as He was then – **the Healer**.

God was going to bring Christ into the world through a descendant of Abraham, but in order to accomplish this it required a **miracle of healing** for Sarah.

We see God once again preserving His people through the miracle of **health** and **healing** while in Egypt and in the wilderness. Psalm 105:37 says 'And there was none feeble among His tribes,' and Psalm 107:20 says, 'He sent His word and healed them . . .'

We can see Christ the Healer in the 10 commandments, 'Honour your father and your mother: that your days may be long . . .' We can see Him in the Law, Deut. 7:12 KJV says, 'Wherefore it shall come to pass, if ye harken to these judgements, and keep, and do them . . . the Lord will take away from them all sickness . . .' Christ the Healer was working among the Kings, Psalm 103:3 says, 'Who forgives all your iniquities: who heals all your diseases . . .' He worked as the Healer during the time of the prophets. Isaiah 53:4 KJV says 'Surely He hath borne our sickness, and carried our pains.' He was there with the apostles all through the Book of Acts and the Epistles. And finally we see Christ the Healer in Revelation, 'And God will wipe away every tear from their eyes: there shall be no more death, nor sorrow, nor crying; and there shall be no more pain, for the former things have passed away' (Rev. 21:4).

Christ the Healer has never changed – He was and is and always will be the **Giver of life** and **health**.

Power to heal, in Christ, in us

Luke 5:17 'And the power of the Lord was present to heal them'

Luke the physician tells us that the power of the Lord was present to heal them, meaning Jesus **wanted to heal**. He was among them to heal, yet only one man, a paralytic was healed. The others failed to recognise His purpose and power.

When the woman with the issue of blood touched Jesus, He said, 'I perceived power going out from Me'. The **healing power** was within Jesus, **available** and **ready** to be released to all who touched Him in faith.

When a leper came to Jesus he said, 'If you are willing, You can make me clean'. How did he know Jesus **could** Heal? Because he saw within Jesus the same characteristic the centurion saw, **the power** and **virtue of life-giving health**.

Mark tells us that Jesus **gave** the disciples power to heal and cast out evil spirits. He could because this power is inherent in Him.

And for what purpose is Christ the embodiment of healing power – to flow out to all mankind, even as His blood did on Calvary. Here Christ was broken to release the divine virtues of God. Here on the rugged cross, heaven's cistern was dashed upon the hard heart of humanity to pour out the fragrance of love. The heavens have opened, like the bleeding side of Christ, and the Spirit with healing in His wings has descended, the water and blood falling to earth. Down it flows, the power from on high, the Holy Spirit, the resurrection and power of Christ now conferred upon His Body, the church.

We are now the healing hands, the hearts of compassion and bearers of glad tidings, declaring, 'The power of the Lord is present to heal'.

Jesus is now saying to us, 'Go in this might of yours,' for as the healing virtue was inherent in Christ it is now inherent in the Church. Let us arise and go forth.

Luke 8:46, Mk. 1:40, Judges 6:14.

Rivers of Healing

Eze. 47:9 'And it shall be that every living thing that moves, wherever the rivers go, will live'.

Jesus said, 'He who believes in Me, as the scripture has said, out of his heart will flow **rivers of living water**'. Those rivers of living water Jesus was talking about were the Holy Spirit.

Wherever the Holy Spirit is flowing, working or present, **life** and **healing** follow. When Naaman the leper dipped 7 times in the **waters** of Jordan he was healed. When the blind man washed his eyes in the **waters** at the pool of Siloam he was healed.

From Genesis to Revelation a **river of life** flows. Genesis 2:10 says, 'Now a **river** went out of Eden to water the gardens.' It was from this river that life came to the new earth. In Revelation 22:1 it says, 'And he showed me a **pure river of water** of **life**, clear as crystal, proceeding **from** the throne of God and of the Lamb. In the middle of its street, and on either side of the **river**, was the tree of life, which bore twelve fruits, each tree yielding its fruit every month. And the leaves of the tree were for the healing of the nations'. It was from this river that **healing** came through the trees.

This is why Jesus sent the Holy Spirit from the Father, to bring us **life** and **health**. The reason the Holy Spirit was upon Jesus was to **heal, deliver**, and **set free**. Jesus **healed** because He was anointed. The New Testament church brought life and healing likewise because of Pentecost.

Paul tells us, 'But if the Spirit of Him who raised Jesus from the dead dwells in you, He who raised Christ from the dead **will also give life** to your mortal **bodies** through His Spirit who dwells in you'.

Does the Holy Spirit dwell in you? Then release those rivers of living water for as Ezekiel said, 'Wherever the rivers go' they bring life, and life means **healing for you**.

John 7:38, Rom. 8:11, Eze. 47:9.

Jesus + Word + Faith = Healing

Ex. 23:25 'And you shall serve the Lord your God, and He will bless your bread and your water. And I will take sickness away from the midst of thee.'

God's will is to **take sickness away from us**. From Genesis to Revelation we see the hand of God healing mankind in many different ways.

Over and over in the gospels we hear Jesus saying 'according to your faith let it be to you' or 'as you have believed so be it done for you'. The centurian's servant was healed because he believed his servant would be healed if Jesus just **spoke the word**. The woman who had an issue of blood believed she would be healed by **touching** Jesus' hem. The **way** some were healed was simply by going to one of the meetings. Others were healed **by** obeying the Lord's specific direction, such as the man with the withered hand who was told to stretch it out.

In the book of Acts we see people healed **by faith in the name of Jesus**, or through the ministry of an evangelist, or the laying on of hands. James tells us people can be healed by the elders of a church, praying the prayer of faith and anointing them with oil in the Name of the Lord.

God has given us various **means** by which we can receive healing so as to meet us at our level of faith. There is only one person who heals, Jesus! And regardless of the method by which we receive it, it must be according to the Word of God and Faith; Jesus the **word of God** and **faith = healing**.

Therefore, which ever avenue you are pursuing to receive healing, whether by standing on His word, having hands laid on you or praying the effectual fervent prayer, see **Jesus** as your Healer and make sure it's according to the Word, and **believe**.

God **wants you to receive. He** is ready to meet you at your level or point of faith and He is saying to you:

Jesus + word of God + faith = healing

Mt. 9:29, Mt. 8:13.

Healing in the Cross

Matthew 8:17 'That it might be fulfilled which was spoken by Isaiah the prophet, saying, Himself took our infirmities, and bore our sicknesses.'

The good news of the gospel is that it is for the whole person: spirit, soul and **body**. Jesus delivers us from **all** our enemies by His work on the cross even as He delivered the Israelites from **all** their enemies when the waters covered the armies of Pharaoh. There is no part of mankind that God has not redeemed unto Himself by Jesus the Lamb, including our **bodies**.

Isaiah foretold the day when Jesus would take our sicknesses upon His body as well as our sins when he said, 'Surely he hath borne our sicknesses (griefs), and carried our pains (sorrows).' David saw the same redemption work when he cried out, 'Who forgiveth all their iniquities, who **healeth all thy diseases**.' And again 'He sent His word and **healed** them, and delivered them from their destruction.' Moses prophesied **healing** in the atonement when all the children of Israel were being bitten by fiery serpents and dying. The Lord said, 'Make a fiery serpent, and set it on a pole, and it shall be that **everyone** who is bitten, when he looks **at it, shall live**.'

Healing is in the **Cross, healing** is in the **atonement, healing** is in **Jesus Christ**. And as we look upon Him in faith we **shall live also**.

Jesus **bore our** sicknesses and **carried our** pains. He **heals all our diseases**. Therefore why should we be bitten by the serpent and die when all we must do is **look to the Healer – Jesus Christ**?

God has already sent His **word**, He has already made atonement (Who His own self bore our sins . . . by whose stripes **ye were healed**). Healing is **now yours. Look** upon the cross this day and **be whole**. He did it for you and me.

Is. 53:4 KJV, Ps. 103:3 KJV, Ps. 107:20, Num. 21:8, 1 Peter 2:23 KJV.

Christ the Healer

Exodus 15:26 'For I am the Lord that healeth thee.'

One day as Smith Wigglesworth (a great British evangelist) was riding home on a train he sat opposite a lady who was ill. After a few minutes of conversation he said to the lady, 'I have a cure in my bag that has never failed.'

You can imagine the hope, excitement and astonishment that must have filled her heart. Then Wigglesworth asked her if she would accept it, and she said yes. At that point he reached into his bag and pulled out his bible and read Exodus 15:26 KJV 'for I am the Lord that healeth thee.' And sure enough, she was healed.

What gave Wigglesworth such confidence that God heals today? He discovered that 'for I am the Lord that healeth thee' is the meaning of one of God's redemptive names, Jehovah – Rapha.

In the Hebrew culture a name was given to describe the person. The name represented the person. And so it is with God. His name declares **who** He is and **what He** is. Therefore when God revealed to the Israelites His name Jehovah-Rapha **He** was revealing **who** He was, **the healer**, and **what He** was, **divine health**.

God is **health** and He is the **healer** which is why, when Jesus came to earth, Peter tells us 'How God anointed Jesus of Nazareth with the Holy Spirit and with power, who went about doing good, and **healing all** who were oppressed of the devil; for God was with Him.

Jesus, who is God, was visibly declaring the name of God, Jehovah-Rapha to the world. And He is still saying there is **healing** in His name today, for the Name of Jesus encompasses **all** the names of God.

Call on His name in faith even as the lame man did at the Gate Beautiful and you will also experience Jesus as Jehovah-Rapha; 'the Lord that **healeth** thee'.

Acts 10:38

Jesus Came to Heal

Psalm 103:2 'Bless the Lord, O my soul, And forget not all His benefits.'

One of God's benefits to us is healing. The following verse to Psalm 103:2 is 'Who forgives all your iniquities, who heals all your diseases.' It says '**All your diseases**.'

Truly healing is a benefit to mankind. Sickness causes pain, suffering, separation, heartache, poverty and even death. But healing brings freedom, joy, life, togetherness and a future.

Jesus came to 'save that which was lost', but he also came, and 'bore our sickness and carried our pains.' James tells us that 'by His stripes we were healed.' Moses declared to Israel that, 'He **is** the **Lord** who **heals you**'. David said, 'He sent His word and **healed them**.' Paul announced that Jesus became a curse for us that we might be **redeemed from** the curse of the law. Listed in Deuteronomy Chapter 28 under the curses of the law is sickness of every kind.

John writes that Jesus came to destroy the works of the devil, and one of his evil works is sickness because Acts 10:38 says, 'God anointed Jesus of Nazareth with the Holy Spirit and power who went about doing **good, healing all** who were oppressed of the devil.'

Sickness is your enemy, Jesus is your **healer**. John 10:10 says 'The thief (the devil) does **not** come except to steal, and to kill and to destroy, but I (Jesus Christ) have come that they may **have life**, and that they may have it more abundantly.' Sickness steals your life, your money, your joy. It can even kill you and it certainly destroys. It destroys bodies, minds, families and futures. But Jesus came to bring **life**, He came to **heal**, to **raise up, to save**.

Say this out loud. **Jesus loves me, He wants me well, He came to give me life, peace and health**. From this day forward see sickness as your enemy and resist it as you would sin. Don't settle for less, stand on God's **word** and the healing that is yours through Christ's atoning work.

Ps 103:3, Mt. 18:11, Mt. 8:17 KJV, Ex. 15:16, Ps. 107:20.

Healing Scriptures

This month the scriptures to meditate, confess and memorise pertain to healing. God wants you whole in spirit, soul and **body**. Psalm 107:20 says, 'He sent His word, and **healed** them, and delivered them from their destruction.' Healing came by the word because the word embodies **the Word**, Jesus Christ the **Healer**. Get these verses into your spirit. They are God's promises to you.

Exodus 15:26 KJV '. . . I am the Lord that **healeth thee**'.

Matthew 8:17 KJV 'That it might be fulfilled which was spoken by Isaiah the prophet, saying **himself** took **our** infirmities, and bore our **sicknesses**.'

1 Peter 2:24 KJV 'Who his own self bore our sins in his own body on the tree, that we, being dead to sins, should live unto righteousness: **by whose stripes ye were healed**.'

Psalm 103:3 KJV 'Who forgiveth all thine iniquities; who **healeth all thy diseases**.'

Acts 10:38 KJV 'How God anointed Jesus of Nazareth with the Holy Spirit and with power; who went about **doing good** and **healing all** that were oppressed of the devil; for God was with Him.'

These are just five scriptures. There are hundreds more. Remember it **is God's** will to heal you.

There are three places in the Bible that reveal God's perfect will:

1. Adam and Eve in the garden.
2. Jesus as he walked the earth.
3. Heaven.

There was no sickness until Adam sinned. Jesus was never sick and in heaven there will be no sickness.

Salvation is an all inclusive word meaning salvation, protection, preservation, wholeness, **healing**. **All** we must do is **accept it, believe it** and **act upon it**. Use this day to strengthen your faith that God wants you well.

Proverbs

1. The child you ignore
   you will soon despise
   A child unnoticed
   will soon bring you shame.

2. Pushing a child aside
   will provoke him to anger
   Drawing the children near
   will evoke him to love.

3. The child of your making
   is an art taught by God

4. To act wisely you must be wise,
   To be a peacemaker, you must
   know the Prince of Peace.

5. An angry father
   will stir a child to anger,
   But a loving mother can
   mend the wounds.

6. Great wealth lies in the heart of a Christian,
   But only a diligent understanding will draw it out.

7. The fear of the Lord brings multiplied blessings;
   But the fear of man brings confusion and compromise.

8. A man of foresight will sow his seed,
   But a man who lacks understanding will eat it.

9. A child who plays in secret
   is a child being trained in deviousness.

10. When choosing a friend listen to the spirit of what he says.

11. What you listen to, you will think upon;
    What you think upon, you will speak about;
    What you speak about, you will soon do.
    Give your ears to the Lord and the righteous mouth;
    Withdraw from the conversation of the wicked and the deceitful
    tongue
    For if you stay and listen, then refuse their ways,
    they will turn on you and desire to bring you to shame.

by D.C.

Heard, Came and Fell

Mk. 7:24–30. vs. 25 'For a woman whose young daughter had an unclean spirit heard about Him, and she came and fell at His feet.'

This is the story of a gentile woman who came to Jesus with a desperate need and walked away with a miracle. What joy must have overflowed from this mother's heart as she saw her daughter delivered from an evil spirit. Her prayers were answered, her hope fulfilled, her faith realized.

But what Jesus did for her was not for her alone, it was simply God revealing His will to man that Jesus has come to give **us** the miracle **we** need. Jesus said 'All that the Father gives Me will come to Me; and the one who comes to Me I will by no means cast out.' Yes, your miracle is waiting for you when you come to Jesus as this Syrophenecian woman did.

First this woman **heard** of **Him**. 'Faith comes by hearing' and the more she heard of Jesus the more she **believed He** could heal her daughter. Take time to **hear** Jesus, read His word and spend time in prayer and, as you do, you will **hear** Him saying, 'As you have believed, **so let it be done for you**.'

Secondly she **came** to Jesus. If we are ever to receive from Jesus, we must draw near to Him. Come boldly into His presence, 'draw near to **God** and He will draw near to you'. 'Enter into His gates with thanksgiving.' Get so close to Jesus that His miracle power becomes your miracle power.

Thirdly she **fell** at His feet. Time and time again we see people receiving miracles because they fell at the feet of Jesus and worshipped Him. When you worship Him you are acknowledging His glory, His majesty, His sovereignty, His Divinity. Worship is a physical and spiritual expression that Jesus is God and is the first love of our life. As this mother was lost in Jesus through worship, her need was met. And so will yours.

Hear Him, come to Him and **worship Him**. This is how she received and this is how **you** will receive also. The miracle is waiting for you.

John 6:37, Rom. 10:17, Mt. 8:13, James 4:8, Ps. 100:4.

Give to Jesus What You Have

Mark 8:4 Then His disciples answered Him, 'How can one satisfy these people with bread here in the wilderness?'

Jesus had just finished a three day revival meeting and the crowds had grown to over 10,000 people. Since no one had expected to be at the meeting so long they soon ran out of food and hunger was now setting in quickly.

It was in this situation that Jesus turned to the disciples and asked them to feed the multitude. To this request the disciples could only respond with, 'How can we satisfy these people with bread here in the wilderness?' It seemed unreasonable. As a matter of fact it seemed impossible!

Does it not seem that our greatest needs come when we are in a desert place? The large bills only come when we have no money. And yet, when we are the weakest that is our opportunity for a **miracle**. When God called Moses to deliver 2½ million Jews, certainly he felt inadequate, insufficient and unqualified, but it was a moment when the **miracle-working power** of God could be revealed.

The secret is to not look at the desert, the need, the barrenness or our inadequacies but to **look to Jesus**. When we do this as the disciples and Moses did then our hopes become visible, our dreams become reality and the impossible becomes possible. It doesn't matter how much we have or don't have but rather it's the **blessing of God** that counts. When Jesus **blessed** the few loaves and fishes they became **more than enough**. When the Spirit of God came upon Moses, Pharaoh and his army were no match for him.

You can release this **miracle** in your life by simply doing what the disciples and Moses did, **give to Jesus what little you have**. God asked Moses, 'What is that in your hand?' It was only a rod, but when put in the hand of God it became a **miracle**. The disciples had to **give** to Jesus the few loaves and fishes before they became a **miracle**.

What is it you have? **Give it to Jesus, let Him bless it and watch a miracle happen**!

Ex. 4:2.

Renew the Mind

Romans 12:2 'And do not be conformed to this world, but be transformed by the renewing of your mind, that you may prove what is that good and acceptable and perfect will of God.'

When a person is born-again their spirit is what is changed into the image and likeness of God. We receive a new nature but our minds are still filled with years of information from our old life. Now we must learn to think God's thoughts and not the world's thoughts. As Paul says, we're to let the mind of Christ be in us and no longer the mind of the world.

In our old life we 'fulfilled the desires of the flesh and of the *mind*.' Now we're to 'set our *mind* on the things above', and fulfill the will of God. If we remain carnaly or fleshly *minded* we will still behave like an unregenerate man. But, if we learn to become spiritually **minded** we will 'walk in the light as He is in the light.'

Though our spirit has been changed, now our minds must be **trained** by the word and the Holy Spirit if we're to live in harmony with ourselves and God.

The Bible says that Lot's righteous soul was vexed by the things he **saw** and **heard**. Lot was constantly placing himself in a position (the gates of Sodom and Gomorrah) where what he **saw** and **heard** was vexing and grieving, depressing his soul. Due to Lot allowing himself to be filled by the things of the world, the light of Christ never shone. The living waters were imprisoned. Today many Christians are vexing their minds by the things they **see** and hear on T.V., radio, in books, magazines, or records, videos and movies and because of this they are never allowing their spirits to grow. This is why they are not being **transformed**, because their *minds* are not being renewed.

We are in a New Kingdom with a New Nature serving a New King and we now need to learn to overcome in Christ. This can happen as we **renew our minds in Christ**. Now we're to meditate on the **word** day and night. Now we're to **set** our **minds on things above**.
We now

Give our attention to (His) words
Incline (our) ears to (His) sayings
Not (letting) them depart from (our) eyes
(But) keeping them in the midst of (our) hearts

Why? For they – The Words of God are **life** and **health**!

Choose life and health today by allowing your mind to be renewed by the word and Spirit.

Phil. 2:5, Eph. 2:3, Col. 3:2, 1 John 1:7, Pr. 4:30–32.

Keeping your mind in Battle

1 Peter 1:13 'Therefore gird up the loins of your mind, be sober, and rest your hope fully upon the grace that is to be brought to you at the revelation of Jesus Christ'.

In this verse Peter is giving us a tried and true, nitty-gritty method of **how to be victorious** in times of testing, trials and persecution. And that is 'gird up the loins of your mind'.

The New English Bible reads 'You must therefore be like men stripped for action, perfectly self-controlled . . .' Moffatt's translation says 'Brace up your minds, then, keep cool,' J.B. Phillips says, 'So brace up your minds, and, as men who know what they are doing . . .' The NIV says, 'Prepare your minds for action: be self-controlled'.

In other words, we must **be** in a state of readiness **before** trials come. As a good student prepares for a test, so must we prepare for the spiritual battle we shall encounter.

Satan loves to give pop quizzes, just to see if we have studied and prepared. I remember the day when working in a restaurant, the space shuttle had broken the sound barrier prior to landing and all the windows in the restaurant vibrated, the noise swept through the building in a crashing boom. The waitress from the carvery came running and in a frantic voice said, 'O mercy, I missed the rapture'. She was easily shaken, needless to say.

Many become disappointed, confused and angered by trials because they have not taken the time to **brace** up their minds with God's word. Isaiah says 'You will keep him in **perfect peace**, Whose **mind** is **stayed** on You'.

We are to take an active part in conditioning, preparing and training ourselves in the work of God for the battles of life. A lazy, dull and confused mind is easy prey for deception. But a mind that meditates **day** and **night** on the word of God is alerted by the Spirit to dangers. We must be ready to **speak** the word at any given moment.

How do we gird up the loins of our mind? By reading, studying, confessing, meditating, memorizing, praying, listening and doing **the word**. For when the word is in your heart and mind it will be that sword of the Spirit, ready to battle.

Is. 26:3.

Proverbs

1. As Samson's sin cut off his hair
   so our sin cuts off the anointing
2. By God changing you
   he could change a million others.
3. By the words of our mouths
   we either build or destroy.
4. When you see your nothingness,
   then turn to God's allness.
   When you feel your inadequacies,
   see God's Almightiness.
   When you think you're worthless,
   behold God's righteousness.
   When there's failure all around,
   identify with God's resurrection.
5. A good salesman will sell you what he likes,
   but the buyer will not know it until he is home.
6. Hasty decisions lead to regrets,
   whereas discretion and waiting upon the Lord bring peace.
7. For one, a crisis leads to success,
   but for another, to his downfall.
8. Honour comes to those who don't look for it,
   but disgrace is the lot of the greedy and selfish.
9. Faith makes a man strong
   but fear brings disaster.
10. A wise man knows how to finish a race,
    but a braggart only knows how to start.
11. It is more blessed to give than to receive,
    yet receiving is fundamental to giving.
12. Sin is like poison:
    they both cause death.
13. There are two things
    that can change the course of a marriage,
    The tears of a woman
    and the anger of a man.

(cont.)

14. There is one thing that makes a husband great,
the respect of his wife.
There is one thing that makes a wife great,
the love of her husband.
There are two things that make children great,
their parents.

15. There is darkness only in the absence of light,
but when light comes, darkness flees.

16. Good hates evil,
and evil hates good.

by D.C.

A Disciplined Race

1 Cor. 9:24–25. '. . . Run in such a way that you may obtain it. And everyone who competes for the prize is temperate in all things . . .'

Paul is likening the Christian life to a race. A race with a prize that is to be won. That prize is the goal or vision, the dream God has given you that He wants you to obtain. But, in order to secure this prize we must 'Run in **such a way**,' we must compete according to the rules.

The first rule for success Paul lays down for us is to be **temperate, self-controlled or disciplined** in **all things**. Everything a runner does during the race will determine whether he receives the prize or not. Therefore the athlete will bring **every aspect** of his life into subjection to the race. He will change his diet, sleeping habits and social life. More and more time and energy will be given to training and activities that are pertinent to winning the race.

So it is with Christians, every area of our lives must come into line and fit into the vision, the goal God has given us. We must learn to 'lay aside every weight, and the sin which so easily ensnares us, and let us run with patience the race that is set before us.' As Solomon said it's the 'little foxes that spoil the vines.' We cannot afford to be sloppy, to make excuses or rationalize certain behaviour that we have not submitted to the Lord.

Jesus set His face like flint towards the cross and **He** never deviated from it. He ran the race and won the prize, you and me.

Now Jesus has passed the torch on to us, and by the Holy Spirit, He will help us run 'in such a way' that we can win also. Therefore let us remember that if anyone competes in athletics, he is not crowned unless he competes **according to the rules**. You **can win** as you allow the Holy Spirit and the Word to make you '**temperate in all things**.'

Heb. 12:1, S. of So. 2:15, 2 Tim. 2:5.

Exercise Resists Death

1 Tim 4:8. 'For bodily exercise profits little'

Many people have taken this to mean that they do not need to exercise, but that is not what Paul is saying. In the margin of the King James it reads 'for a little time.' Our bodies will function on an average from 70–80 years and in the light of eternity it is 'for a little time.'

Too many Christians have allowed their bodies to 'get away from them' and have used this verse as an excuse. However, though exercise 'profiteth little', it does profit to some extent.

God's salvation for man is for the **whole** person; spirit, soul and **body**. On numerous occasions we are told that our body is the temple of the Holy Spirit, that we are to glorify God in our body as well as spirit. Paul said that he would keep his body in subjection to himself and the Lordship of Christ.

Our bodies have now become **instruments** for God, they are a means by which the Lord can minister Life to the world. As I was running one day the Lord spoke to me and said, 'When you exercise you are resisting the devil.' It is always exciting when God speaks to you but this was a particular blessing because it gave me purpose to exercise. I began to see that death is working in my body, it is getting older every day. Yet as I exercise I am resisting the force of death. I am restraining its effect upon me.

Paul said 'Run that you may obtain.' Running in the physical helps my body be more responsive to my spirit. When you exercise, it is easier to rise up early in prayer. You can work more effectively and be more productive.

Declare to your body today that Jesus is Lord. Begin to see your bulges as your enemies, out to sap your life and slow you down. Resist them, even as you would resist sin, and exercise to win for the glory of God.

1 Cor. 9:24 KJV.

Labour is not in Vain in Christ

1 Cor. 15:58 'Therefore, my beloved brethren, be steadfast, immovable, always abounding in the work of the Lord, knowing that your labour is not in vain in the Lord.'

Work is basic to the Christian faith, for without it nothing would get done. Yet the very nature of work sometimes inhibits us from working. It's hard and unending, it takes concentration, determination of will and physical energy. Possibly everyone felt as Solomon did from time to time when he said, 'Vanity of vanities, all is vanity. What profit has a man from all his labour in which he toils under the sun?'

Paul, however, discovered the reason that enabled him to work tirelessly and joyfully for the Lord.

1. Paul said, 'Knowing that your labour is **not in vain in the Lord**.' Paul worked with purpose, meaning and direction. He knew **why** he was working and **what** he was trying to accomplish. He found Christ to be his purpose, his director, his way and his end. Christ was the beginning and end of his labour.

2. Paul states in the verse previous to 1 Cor. 15:58 'But thanks be to God, who gives **victory** through our Lord Jesus Christ'. *Therefore* we can be **steadfast, immovable, always abounding**. Paul knew his labour would bear the fruit of **victory**. In Christ his labour reaped success, not failure. He accomplished his goal, it wasn't wasted time or effort. We, like Paul, are motivated always when we can **see** the victory at the end of the road. Paul saw this in Christ.

3. 1 Corinthians 15:10 says, 'But by the grace of God I am what I am; and His grace towards me was not in vain; but I laboured more abundantly than they all: yet not I but the grace of God which was with me.' Paul found the grace of God his source of strength to, '**press** towards the goal', '**fight** the good fight of faith', '**work** for the night is coming.' Paul's sufficiency came from God, an unending source of power, purpose, drive and direction.

Ecc. 1:2–3, 1 Cor. 15:58, 1 Cor. 15:57, Phil. 3:14, 1 Tim. 6:12.

Run to Win and Taking Possession

Numbers 13:30 'Let us go up at once and take possession for we are well able to overcome it'.

The difference between success and failure is our determination to win or our fear of failure.

God's desire for us is to run to win, to accomplish the task, to take the prize. Paul writes, 'Know ye not that they which run in a race run all, but one receiveth the prize. So run **that ye may obtain**'. Paul was expressing the same faith as Caleb was when he said, 'Let us **go** up at once and **take possession**, for we are well able to overcome it'. They saw the prize and they both determined that in Christ they could win.

The Israelites who were running the race with Caleb, however, did not have the same perception of the prize. They said, 'The walls are too high, the giants too big, the armies too strong and they will surely eat us alive'. Their fear of the competition caused them to prepare for defeat. They gave up the race and turned back.

In our Christian walk there are many opportunities for fear, discouragement, failure and self-pity if we allow the competition to intimidate us. But if like Caleb and Paul we keep our eyes on the prize, victory will rise up out of our spirit. When the devil threw his best at Job, what do we hear? 'I know that my Redeemer lives.' When David was surrounded by enemies we hear these words from the midst of the battle 'Blessed be the Lord my rock, who trains my hands for war, And my fingers for battle. He makes my feet like feet of a deer, And sits me on my **high** places, For by You I have run against a troop, and **BY MY GOD** I can leap over a wall'.

The prize winners can be heard on every page of the Bible, from every walk of life, in every possible circumstance of living. And your name can be added to these clouds of witnesses also as you pick up the torch and begin to run to win!

1 Cor. 9:24 KJV, Job. 19:25, Ps. 144:1, 18:33, 29.

Drawing Near

Psalm Twenty Seven

You have said 'come unto Me',
 and I have said, 'I will come.'
O the joy of hearing Your voice.
Your words of light and power,
 how they pierce the centre of my soul
 and fill me with Your Holy strength.

To You, O Lord, I draw near,
 holding fast to the Cross,
 and living by Your Throne.
How high and lifted up You have carried me,
 Your joint-heir, Your living body.

To You, O Lord, I ever press on,
 letting nothing stop or turn me away.
I run, I race, I push and press to You alone
 my Saviour Divine.
What grace You have brought to my heart.

Faith You give to run the race.
Courage and boldness to ride the winds.
What trial, mountain, lion, or demon
 can stand before Your victory,
 Your victory in me.

by D.C.

To Obey is Better than Sacrifice

2 Sam: To obey is better than sacrifice.

Sacrificing is a mark of Christianity, but we must be careful that it doesn't become religious. Solomon said 'To do righteousness and justice is **more** acceptable to the Lord than sacrifice.' Jesus said through the Psalmist's mouth 'sacrifice and offering you did not desire; But a body You have prepared for Me. In burnt offerings and sacrifices for sin You had no pleasure. Then I said, "Behold, I have come – In the volume of the Book it is written of Me – To do **your will, O God**" .'

Obedience and right living is what pleases the Father more than sacrifices. The Father was more pleased with His Son's obedience and willing heart than he was with the actual sacrifice. Why? Because God looks upon the heart, and the condition of our heart is **more** important to Him than outward sacrifices. When Jesus walked the earth the priests offered many sacrifices to God but what did Jesus say, 'I desire mercy and not sacrifice.'

It was the willing obedience of Jesus that made his sacrifice efficacious and acceptable, and it is the condition of **our** hearts that makes any sacrifices acceptable unto God also.

Isaiah 1:19 says 'If you are **willing** and **obedient** you shall eat the good of the land.' If we want our sacrifices of giving, praise, fasting and time to have God's divine approval upon them then it will be through a **heart** that is **willing** and **obedient**.

Religion **demands** sacrifice, God **inspires** it. Don't allow yourself to get caught up with religious **routines**, the **'letter killeth**, but the **spirit giveth life**.' **Remember, Christianity is a relationship, not a religion**. Stay sensitive to the Holy Spirit and walk as He leads you by the Word. Then, any sacrifice that is required will be a **joy** rather than a lonesome task.

Pr. 21:3, Heb. 10:5–7, Mt. 9:13.

Desire for His Will

Ps. 119:35 'Make me walk in the path of Your commandments, for I delight in it'.

There is a secret to obedience, and it is having a greater **desire** to do the Father's will than to follow the desires of our flesh. How does one get such a desire? From the Holy Spirit.

Many Christians attempt to obey the Lord by the flesh. They want to obey, they resolve to obey, they attempt and decide to obey but it's still **self-effort**. And as long as self is involved in our obedience, we shall fail.

The lesson that must be learned is that **we** cannot live the life of Christ, **only the Holy Spirit can**. Galatians 5:16 says A.B. 'But I say, walk and live habitually in the (Holy) Spirit – responsive to and controlled and guided by the Spirit' then you will certainly not gratify the cravings and desires of the flesh – of human nature without God'.

God wants us to discover that alone **we** cannot obey Him, and then ask Him to help us incline, predispose or move our hearts by His Spirit to **want** to obey Him.

When **we** are trying to keep His word we end up in the conflict Paul talks about in Romans 7:15, 'For what I am doing, I do not understand. For what I will to do, that I do not practice, but what I hate, that I do'. We want to obey God, but how often do we disobey? As long as the **wanting-to-obey** comes from our flesh it will be tossed to and fro by every wind of craving, circumstance and personal preference. But when the flesh is out of the picture and the Holy Spirit is **wanting-to-obey** in us, then the question of obedience is resolved. We now triumph in Christ.

Is there freedom from self-want? **Yes**! Paul writes, 'And those who are Christ's have crucified the flesh **with** its passions and **desires**'. Yes, even our desire to serve the Lord has been crucified and the Holy Spirit can **now desire in us**. This is the fundamental change from failure to success, it's going from **self-desire to Holy Spirit-desire**.

Obedience or Success?

L.B. Mark 10:44 'And whoever wants to be greatest of all must be the slave of all'.

Maintaining a life of victory in Christ Jesus means never allowing success to take precedence over obedience.

Jesus moved in miraculous power because He trusted the Holy Spirit and the Holy Spirit trusted Him. The Hebrew writer tells us that Jesus was **obedient 'even unto the death on the cross**.' Jesus **always** obeyed the guidance of the Spirit, regardless of the consequences.

In John Chapter 6, Jesus had just fed well over five thousand people with only a few fish and loaves of bread. It was a miracle that astonished the people. And because of such a miracle the crowds loved Him. They elected to make Him King. Here, at a moment of true success when the world was in His hands, the Bible says, He sent the multitudes away and 'departed again to a mountain by Himself alone.' In obedience to the Holy Spirit He left popularity, wealth, comfort and a secure pastoral job.

After a day of many healings, miracles and crowds, Jesus turns to His disciples and tells them of His death. Just when everyone was feeling good and the ministry was going well, when it seemed as if Jesus was the Messiah taking His Kingdom, He very clearly reminds them – He must suffer and die.

Jesus never allowed success to determine His path, He never used it as a barometer to judge His spirituality or ministry.

The disciples learned the same lesson after Pentecost. Philip was holding a city-wide revival with multitudes being healed, saved and delivered, but when the Spirit told him to go and minister to *one* man, in the desert, He obeyed. He left the crowds, offerings, success, popularity and appeals.

A victorious Christian **knows** that Jesus is the way, not success. Success must be the servant, it must follow. It must not be the master or motive.

Phil. 2:8 KJV, John 6:15, 1 Cor. 3:21–22, 1 Cor. 3:23.

Obedience, the door to Miracles

Romans 5:19 'For as by one man's disobedience many were made sinners, so also by one Man's obedience many were made righteous.'

While sitting on the platform of a particular church where I was conducting a weekend of meetings, I became aware in my spirit that the anointing of prophecy was upon the pastor's wife. I looked up at her and was waiting for her to give the message. Several minutes passed by and then she spoke out in tongues.

When she had finished I stood up and gave the interpretation, which in essence was, 'I am anointing this church with the spirit of prophecy. You are to be the prophetic voice and forerunner in this community to my people. You are the spearhead that will lead the way of what I am doing in My Body in this area'.

That night this church was released into a new dimension and experienced a breakthrough. And it all happened **because of this woman's obedience**. Since God had annointed her she was the key link in the chain that released God's prophetic gift to the whole local church. If she had not responded and obeyed the Holy Spirit, there would have been no breakthrough that night.

In Mark chapter 10, we read of a rich young ruler who came to Jesus wanting a breakthrough also. He asked Jesus, 'What must I do to be saved?' Jesus answered him, 'One thing you lack. Go your way, sell whatever you have and give to the poor, take up your cross, and follow Me.' This rich young ruler failed to **obey** and so failed to break through.

It is through the **obedience** of one, Christ Jesus, that many have experienced the grace of God. And it will be through our **simple obedience** that breakthroughs and **miracles** will be released into our lives and the lives of others. We are all **links in a chain of God's eternity** and as **we obey**, the key will unlock the door of miracles. You may be an Ananias to Paul or a Peter to Cornelius, a servant girl to Naaman or a man carrying a pitcher of water to the disciples.

Mk. 10:21.

In The Right Place To Hear

Jeremiah 18:2 'Arise and go down to the potter's house, and there I will cause you to hear My words.'

There are times when we have to be in the right place to **hear** God. Jeremiah was told to go to the potter's house before he would **hear** any further instructions. Elijah went on a 40 day journey to a cave in a mountain before he **heard** once again from the Lord. Jesus had to go up the mountain to experience transfiguration. The Apostles were told to go and wait in Jerusalem **until** they received the Holy Spirit.

Hearing from God starts with obedience, and obedience will then release God into your lives. We have all heard Christians say at some time 'God doesn't speak to me,' or 'I never hear the voice of God.' It is not that God is not speaking to us but that we are not in the right **place** to hear Him.

What we need to do is to remember what God spoke to us last and then **obey it**. This will then **put us in the right place to hear further instructions.**

God told Abraham to go into the Land of Canaan, and once being in Canaan God continued to speak to him more and more. God is asking you to take those steps of faith also and put yourself in the right place to hear him. Is He calling you to pray at a certain hour? Is He calling you to search the Word of God? Is there a Canaan to which He has called you?

Your obedience will bring the blessing! Your being in the right place at the right time will bring the answer. Like Jeremiah you may not know what He is going to say, but whenever **God speaks, life comes**! You have never had this day before and you will never have it again. **Now** is your opportunity. Launch out into the deep as Peter did at the Lord's command and you will **hear the answer**!

Remove the Thornbushes

Reading: Mark 4:3–20

The Word-seed that God has sent to earth is **perfect** seed 'In the beginning was the Word, and the Word was with God, and the Word was God'. And it was by this perfect Word-seed that we were born again, 'having been born again, not of corruptible seed but incorruptible, through the word of God which lives and abides forever'.

Therefore in this parable of the sower sowing the seed we know that the problem is **not** with the seed (for it's the infallible word of God) but with the soil (our heart). The fruit we bear then is not a reflection of the seed or word but the condition of our hearts.

Jesus says, 'But these are the ones sown on **good ground**, those who hear the word, accept it and bear fruit: some thirtyfold, some sixty and some a hundred'. Good seed in **good** ground **will** produce fruit, but good seed in poor ground produces little or no fruit.

Ask yourself this question, 'Am I producing as much fruit as I desire or what God would want of me?' If not, then don't be discouraged but rejoice, for in this parable Jesus is revealing to us the pathway to fruitful Christian lives. All we must do is begin to **remove the thornbushes from our soil**.

This is how the Word-seed will spring up through our heart-soil, by clearing away the rocks, thorns, weeds and insects. By repenting, forgiving, forgetting and forfeiting **anything** that hinders the growth of the Word-seed within us.

As good farmers, look upon your fields once again and examine the fruit in relation to the seed you have been sowing. And if the fruit is less than should be expected, be honest. Don't blame God, His Word, the weather or life. Look at your life, your heart, your ground and allow the Holy Spirit to help you renew the ground.

The seed is good, God planted it to produce fruit. Don't allow yourself to be cheated or robbed any longer. **Remove the thornbushes today** and **grow**!

John 1:1, 1 Peter 1:23, Mk. 4:20.

Proverbs

1. When you listen to one side of an argument,
   Remember, there is always another side.

2. History has proven
   that we do not learn from history.
   One generation proves the former
   generation to be wrong and them to be right.
   Satan has taught us
   that pride comes before a fall
   and sin separates.
   Nature has shown
   there are exceptions to exceptions,
   The man who boasts in his strength
   has shown us that even he must die.
   A woman of beauty has forewarned
   us that old age comes to everyone.
   Youth has taught us that zeal is not the answer.
   Death has taught us that we are but dust.
   Old age has taught us that life is just a breath.
   God has taught us that Jesus is the Way,
   the Truth and the Life.

3. Every task is to be an exercise in prayer.

by D.C.

Grace Overcomes

Genesis 6:8 'But Noah found grace in the eyes of the Lord.'

In the days of Noah the earth was corrupt and filled with violence. Its wickedness and sin was so great that the Lord was sorry for ever making man.

Yet in the midst of all the violence and crime, the degradation and sin, Noah and his family were protected. Even though they were the **only** family in **all** the earth that were righteous, they **overcame** sin because they found **grace** in God's eyes.

Jesus said that in the last days it would be even as in the days of Noah. Today we can see that violence and war have once again filled the earth. Crime, immorality, terrorism and ungodliness are affecting every nation.

Yet Paul writes 'where sin abounds, **grace** does much more abound'. As in the days of Noah sin is abounding, but even more important, **grace is much more abundant**, and its **abundance is for you**.

The media, newspapers and magazines are continually reporting the sins of mankind but, like Noah and Paul, we can discern that God's **grace** is **sufficient** to preserve us 'in the midst of a crooked and perverse generation'. The sin that abounded in the Roman Empire could not stop the early church from growing because, 'great **grace** was upon them all'. Regardless of the sin that was in our lives we were saved by **grace**.

Despite the decline of mankind's condition, we are **overcomers** for 'sin **shall not** have dominion over us, for we are not under law but under **grace**.' **We** do not have to fear but only walk by faith in God's grace 'for by **grace** we are **saved** through faith, and that not of yourselves; it is a gift of God.'

Rom. 5:20 KJV, Phil. 2:15, Acts 4:33, Rom. 6:14, Eph. 2:8.

The Power of Grace

Eph. 4:7 'But to each one of us grace was given according to the measure of Christ's gift'.

Grace is all of God's goodness, mercy, love and kindness extended toward us through Jesus Christ, Grace is that quality of God that **enables** and **allows** us to accomplish His will in our lives. This is why Paul begins every epistle with **grace to you** and ends every epistle with **grace be with you**. It was as though Paul wanted to surround everything he said to the saints with **grace**.

Paul understood that everything he was and everything he did was by the **grace** of God in Christ Jesus. Paul writes 'I became a minister according to the gift of **grace** of God . . .', and again, **'To me**, who am less than the least of all the saints, His **grace was given . . .'**

Luke tells us the reason for the early church's phenomenal growth and powers in Acts 4:33 'And **great grace** was upon them all'. It was also Luke who tells us that Jesus 'grew and became strong in spirit, filled with wisdom; and the **grace** of God was **upon** Him'. (Luke 2:40) The life and work of Jesus was **because of grace**. He was **God's grace made visible**. Noah was another one who, having found **grace** in the eyes of the Lord, escaped the destruction of mankind and became the new father of the human race.

Grace is God's declaration of independence, granting us life, liberty and the pursuit of happiness as well as the Bill of Rights proclaiming liberty and justice for all.

Grace is **not** a meagre sustaining in the time of trouble, but rather the enablement of God to **fulfil** His will. It was the grace of God that raised Jesus from the dead, that caused Paul to say 'I have finished the race,' that has preserved the Jewish nation over the centuries. And it is **grace** that will release the whole of God into our situation also. God's grace is sufficient, God's grace is **abounding**; God's grace is His free gift to us. Let us therefore 'be strong in the grace that is in Christ Jesus'. For it is God's gift of overcoming power to us today.

Eph. 3:7–8, 2 Tim. 4:7, 2 Tim. 2:1.

Proverbs

1. An angry woman is as death
   to a soul.
   But a woman of grace is as sunlight
   to a morning glory.

2. Every sunrise is a foretaste
   of Christ's resurrection.

3. As sleep is to the body,
   So is prayer to the soul.

4. As day follows night,
   So are the sure mercies of our
   covenant-keeping God.

5. Take your hand off the helm,
   And the ship has lost its course.
   Take your heart off the Lord,
   And your life is soon dashed upon the
   rocks.

6. The rich and the poor accuse each other
   alike of wasteful living.

7. Knowledge of right and wrong comes
   by intimate fellowship with the Lord.

by D.C.

Husbands and Wives

Ephesians 5:31 'And they two shall be one flesh'

Husbands see the general picture,
  Wives see the details.
Husbands like to think they are right,
  But wives know they are.
Reasoning is the husbands' pride,
  The wives' pride their emotions.
Husbands are the head of the house,
  But wives are their equal.
Husbands shout
  and wives cry.
Husbands hand down the law,
  And wives dress it with grace.
Yet man runs after woman
  And woman runs away;
And when the race is finally over
  they wrestle to their death.
It's the only way to become one!

Overcoming differences in marriage comes as each person dies in Christ and is resurrected in **His** image and in **His** likeness. Then, once we are joined to the Lord it is now Christ living in each spouse. Weaknesses become strengths and wrongs are forgiven, joys are shared and goals become one. In Christ the two become one because we are now bone of His **bone**, flesh of His **flesh**, and **He** is living in both as **one**. Only in this way is Christ the **centre** of the marriage and the marriage is the **outflowing** of **Christ's life**.

To the Least of These

Matt. 25:40,45 'Assuredly, I say to you, inasmuch as you did it to one of the least of these My brethren, you did it to Me'. 'Assuredly, I say to you, inasmuch as you did not do it to one of the least of these, you did not do it to Me'.

The way we treat our brothers and sisters in the Body is **exactly the way we treat Jesus**.

In the Epistle to the Ephesians it says husbands are to love their wives **just as** Christ loved the church and **gave** Himself for it. Wives are to submit to their husbands **just as** the church is subject to Christ. We are to forgive one another **just as** God forgave us in Christ. John tells us we are to love one another **as** Christ loved the church. We're to lay down our lives for each other **because** Christ laid down His life for us. The parallel is continuously drawn between our relationship to one another and our relationship to Christ. By learning to see our spouses, children and fellow Christians as members of Christ, then our attitudes, thoughts and behaviour toward them will change. Paul wrote, 'And if one member suffers, all the members suffer with it; or if one member is honoured all the members rejoice with it.' Why? Because verse 27 says, 'Now you are the body of Christ, and members individually.'

We cannot say we have no need of a hand or foot, eye or ear. As the Body of Christ we need every part. Romans 12:4–5 says, 'Just as there are many parts to our bodies, so it is with Christ's body. We are all parts of it, and it takes every one of us to make it complete . . .'

By seeing each other in this light we can **overcome** every vicissitude of life, for we shall care for others as we would care for Jesus.

A prayer:

Precious Father, teach me how to love your Son, to bind up His wounds and comfort His heart when broken. To embrace Him after a long, hard day's work and reach out in compassion when He has scraped His knee from falling off a bicycle. To bring Him flowers and help with the dishes. To take Him in when He has nowhere to stay. To bring out the best of my clothes when His are worn and tattered. To visit Him when sick and in prison. To give Him my time when He's grown old, and to understand Him when others have turned Him away. Help me to see them as Jesus.
Amen.

1 Cor. 12:26.

You are Needed

2 Cor. 1:20 'For all the promises of God in Him are Yes, and in Him Amen, to the glory of God through us.'

To think of ourselves as insignificant is wrong thinking, because God has declared in His word that He will **not** work independently of us. In this verse 2 Cor. 1:20 He tells us that **all** of the promises come to pass **through us**. God has chosen His plans, purposes and will to be worked out **through man**. Ephesians 3:20 says, 'Now to Him who is able to do exceedingly abundantly above all that we ask or think, according to the power that works **in us**.' God is working out His great master plan of love **through everyday people like you and me**.

The promise of the Messiah was fulfilled **through** a human vessel, Mary. The salvation of mankind is being carried out **through the church**. Even God came to earth in the form of a man, Jesus worked in His human body.

We are important, we are significant, we are of great value to the Father. We are the **body of Christ the head**. This means whatever the **head** desires to do, it will **do it through the body – you**.

If you were to stay in bed all day instead of going to work, how much would you accomplish? Nothing. You can think about work all day long but until your **body** actually does the work, nothing will happen. This is why the **thoughts of Christ become our action**, so His will in heaven will be done on earth.

We are chosen, we are **God-ordained, indispensible living stones to the building of His Kingdom, to the fulfilment of all His promises**.

Today, in your life, God's divine destiny is being worked out. You are needed!